Birds
in my mustard tree
how to grow your faith

Susanne Scheppmann

randall house
114 Bush Rd | Nashville, TN 37217
randallhouse.com

Birds in My Mustard Tree
© 2008 by Susanne Scheppmann

Published by Randall House
114 Bush Road
Nashville, TN 37217

Printed in the United States of America

ISBN 10: 0892656689
ISBN 13: 9780892656684

To My Husband, Mark,

You mirror the love of God. Your goodness and kindness have helped me to comprehend that my mustard seed faith can rest assured in our majestic God. My faith blossoms as I travel this journey of faith beside you. Thank you for loving me as Christ loved the Church.

Love,

Susanne

Table of Contents

Thank you, my Cellophane Friends who on Tuesday night wrapped me in clear authenticity, love, and laughter. Each of you encouraged me in a variety of ways as I wrote this study on faith.

Afi—perseverance
Becky—gentleness
Heidi—faithfulness
Lisa—love
Judi—kindness
Sandra—patience

But the fruit of the Spirit is love, joy, peace, patience, kindness, goodness, faithfulness, gentleness and self-control. Against such things there is no law.
Galatians 5:22-23

Thank you, Michelle Orr, my tireless editor who took on this book project in mid-stream, you played a vital role in refining the final product. Bless you!

I thank my God every time I remember you.
Philippians 1:3

Thank you, Mark, for all of your love. Without you, this book would not have been written. You are a living example of Ephesians 5:25.

Husbands, love your wives, just as Christ loved the church and gave himself up for her.

Finally, to my Lord Jesus Christ, may this study bring honor to your faithful Name.

Your kingdom is an everlasting kingdom,
and your dominion endures through all generations.
The Lord is faithful to all his promises
and loving toward all he has made.
Psalm 145:13

Why write a study on the topic of faith?

My own faith wavers. Some days I trust God with all my heart, mind, and soul. But then there are those other days—times when life's circumstances make my faith shake, rattle, and roll. Doubt arises. Storms of life howl and shake my wobbly faith. I ask myself, "Is my faith ever going to grow beyond the size of a mustard seed?"

I wrote *Birds in My Mustard Tree* as an encouragement for myself and others. I wanted to remind myself and share with others the fact that God does not expect us to become "giants of faith" overnight. God looks beyond our unfaithfulness and our faithlessness. He sees our faith as a seed that grows and blossoms throughout our entire lives.

In addition, God does not want us to feel guilty about our faith. He desires that each of us have an excited anticipation about who He is and how He works in our lives every day. *Birds in my Mustard Tree* is a study to help each of us realize the truth of 2 Timothy 2:13a, "If we are faithless, He will remain faithful." Our God will take our small seed of faith and grow it into a remarkably solid faith. Our growing faith will prove the goodness and faithfulness of the God we serve—Jesus Christ—to the entire world.

Susanne

Week 1
Mustard Seed Faith

Day 1 – **I Can't See You!**

Lord,

I yearn for more faith—faith to believe in You. However, I am not sure what the term faith entails. I hear it thrown around from conversation to conversation. Today, give me a glimpse of what it means when I ask to have faith in You.

In Jesus' name, Amen

This week I am boarding a plane to fly across the country to speak at a women's event. Frightening things can happen to planes. Engine failure might occur. Terrorists plot to explode planes in midair. Every traveler waits in tedious security lines to drop the clear baggy packed liquids into a plastic bin, remove their shoes and jackets, then proceed through the newest security machine. Air travel oozes with the sense of danger.

However, I am going to board the plane. I trust the TSA officials will screen all boarding passengers for potential explosives. I have faith that the pilot is licensed and capable of flying the jumbo jet. I will cram into my seat along with three hundred other passengers who trust the plane will land at its intended destination.

So why do I have faith in all of this? I don't know. I can't explain it rationally. Although I can trust a several ton metal object to fly, yet I struggle with how to

NOW FAITH is the assurance (the confirmation, the title deed) of the things [we] hope for, being the proof of things [we] do not see and the conviction of their reality [faith perceiving as real fact what is not revealed to the senses].
Hebrews 11:1, AMP

The fundamental fact of existence is that this trust in God, this faith, is the firm foundation under everything that makes life worth living. It's our handle on what we can't see. Hebrews 11:1, MSG

Faith assures us of things we expect and convinces us of the existence of things we cannot see. Hebrews 11:1, GW

place my faith in the God that I know and love. Now does that make any sense? Absolutely not, but do you struggle with placing your faith in God?

If yes, then throughout this study your struggling faith will learn to grow. If your faith is as small as a mustard seed, that's okay. God will tend and water it until it is large enough for the results of your faith to be evident to others. Your mustard seed faith will branch out to hold the results of great faith – birds in your mustard tree.

How would you define the term *faith*?

_____

When some of my more faith-filled friends urge me, "Just have faith. It will all work out." I want to yell, "Explain faith to me, please!" So, what we are going to do today is attempt to get a grasp on the concept of faith.

Please read Hebrews 11:1 and then rewrite the verse in your own words:

_____

_____

How did your original definition of faith and the description of faith in Hebrews 11:1 line-up?

_____

_____

My explanation of the term *faith* relates to the idea of *trust*. I looked up the terms *faith* and *trust* in the dictionary. Although similar, they have a distinct difference because *faith* infers trusting in something unseen. Hmmm . . . Let's look at a few different versions of Hebrews 11:1 to see if Scripture confirms this idea of trusting in an unseen God. Read the various versions of Hebrews 11:1 in the margin.

Scripture points to the fact that faith is trusting without seeing. I guess it's similar to my faith that the pilot knows how to fly a jumbo jet. But let's examine Hebrews 11 a bit more because it gives us examples of people who had faith in God. In fact, Hebrews 11 is often referred to as the "Heroes of Faith" chapter.

Read Hebrews 11:1-31 and then match the correct person with his or her action of faith.

Abel	Kept the Passover
Enoch	Blessed Jacob and Esau about the future
Rahab	Hid the spies
Noah	Blessed Joseph's sons
Moses	Built an ark
Jacob	Offered God a better sacrifice
Isaac	Did not experience death

All of these people held faith in a physically invisible God. Each of them acted in faith concerning an unknowable future. Abel offered a better sacrifice than Cain. Enoch pleased God and, as a result, did not experience death. Isaac and Jacob trusted God with the future of their sons. Noah built an ark to save his family. (A small side note – it had never rained on earth yet.) Rahab hid spies and thus saved her life. Moses kept the Passover and the sprinkling of blood by faith that God would not destroy the firstborn of Israel.

Now let's take a closer look at Abraham; his faith astonishes me. List what he did by faith.

Verse 8: _____

Verse 9: _____

Verse 11: _____

Verse 17: _____

This fellow left home to go to an unknown country and settle down with his wife, Sarah. (I think Sarah must have possessed some trust here too.) By faith, they prepared a nursery instead of preparing for a nursing home. Finally, God commanded the ultimate act of faith. He asked Abraham to sacrifice his only son, Isaac. Abraham reacted in obedience to the command. Abraham's faith proved true, as he knew God would somehow come through because of His faithfulness. And God did; He provided a ram for the sacrifice.

How did God increase Abraham's faith to the point that he could offer his son, Isaac, as a sacrifice? God built it through one incident of trust at a time. Author Jennifer Kennedy Dean explains Abraham's faith as,

> He lined up every truth he knew, stacked them one on top of the other, and then reached the only possible conclusion. He took inventory of everything that had already been proven true. He put the present call of God into his inventory.
>
> Abraham lined up the facts he knew and deduced from what he did not know...To get to faith—obeying the present voice—Abraham reasoned. He reached a conclusion about what he could not see based on what he had already seen. He reasoned that God could raise the dead. That became fact and reality to him when he put it to the test.[1]

Do you believe that faith was easy for any of the historical figures? Why or why not? What doubts do you think passed through Abraham's thoughts?

_____

_____

Did you notice most of the verses in Hebrews began with the phrase, "By faith"? Let's see how our own chapter of faith might read. Fill in the phrase from your own faith experiences.

By faith _____, in the past believed that God
　　　　　　(Your name)

_____.

By faith _____, is believing God for _____.
　　　　　　(Your name)

By faith _____, will believe that _____.
　　　　　　(Your name)

Well, my friend, we learned that faith is trusting in an unseen God. But as we close today's lesson, check out what God provided for us so we can "see" God's character, attributes, and emotions. Write out the following verses that refer to Jesus Christ.

John 1:14:

_____

_____

Hebrews 1:3:

_____

_____

How did God provide the world with a visual image of Himself?

_____

Jesus is the exact representation of God. Tomorrow, we are going to learn about following Jesus Christ by faith. Take a moment and pray for God to increase your "by faith."

Dear God,

In Your name, Amen

Faith Fun
Make a list of five things you put your faith and trust in which might seem absurd. For example: jumbo jets, brain surgeons, etc.

1. _____

2. _____

3. _____

4. _____

5. _____

Faith Finale!
The Word became flesh and made his dwelling among us. We have seen his glory, the glory of the One and Only, who came from the Father, full of grace and truth.
John 1:14

13

Day 2 – O', Come, All Ye Faithless

Jesus,

Begin to grow my faith. Open my eyes to how You grew faith in Your disciples. Allow my faith to bud as I recall how You have already worked miracles in my own life.

In Your name, Amen

I own two small dogs. They trust me to care for them and provide for their needs. This hasn't always been the case. When they were puppies, I had to train them to trust and obey me. This proved difficult, if not impossible, when I gave a command and no type of reward followed. But, if I rewarded them for their faith in me, they soon began to behave eagerly in the conduct I desired. I would hold a tasty treat in one hand and then give a command for a desired behavior. When they obeyed, they were rewarded with a treat. They learned to trust my voice and my instruction. Eventually, I could call them to "come" and they would bound toward me whether or not a dog biscuit awaited. They had learned through my patience and kindness they could have faith in me as their owner.

Faith Fiction
God always increases our faith through boring and mouth-yawning, monotonous regimens.

God works the same way with us. I know it's an unflattering picture for us to be compared to dogs. However, I believe God trains us with patience and kindness and rewards us as we begin our walk of faith with Him, in much the same way we teach our puppies. Let's take a look at how men and women who knew nothing about the man, Jesus, gave up everything to follow Him. He called the faithless and taught them to trust Him.

Read Luke 5:1-11. In verse 2 what were the two fishermen doing?

_____

What did Jesus request Simon to do?

_____

How did Simon respond?

_____

How did Jesus reward his obedience?

_____

How did Peter and the other anglers react to the large number of fish?

_____

In verse 11 what resulted from their astonishment of Jesus?

_____

Visualize for a moment the scene. The fishermen were discouraged by the lack of fish, and they still needed to clean the nets. Up strolls Jesus and asks if He could use their boat for a small conference session offshore. The disciples probably thought, "Sure. Why not? It isn't any good for fishing."

After Jesus finishes His life-coaching session, He tells the men to "Put out into deep water and let down the nets for a catch" (Luke 5:4). (Remember, by now the men had probably cleaned their nets and put them away.) Peter reminds Jesus they have fished all night, but haven't brought in any fish. Somewhat reluctantly, the men do what Jesus asks. The reward for their small faith? A catch of fish so large it began to break the net! Their faith increases and they follow Him.

Because Jesus grows our faith in individual ways, it's unlikely our experience with a miraculous event will be a boatload of fish. My first miraculous event was the act of love presented by my stepmother who loved me when I was an unlovable, stringy-haired, sullen adolescent. She displayed the love of Christ through a variety of ways—homemade cinnamon rolls, carving pumpkins, and talking to me about the love of God. Her love for me brought my faith to fruition and it developed into a small kernel. I barely held enough faith to believe that there was a God, let alone that He loved me enough to die on the cross for me. Through a mustard seed prayer, I asked Jesus to become a part of my life. Then with a faith that wavered most of the time, I began to follow Him.

What is your story of coming to faith in an unseen God? Write a few sentences about the process. Can you see some type of miracle involved?

_____

_____

_____

_____

If you haven't made this life-changing decision, but would like to do so now, it is a very simple process. Just as Simon Peter said, "I am a sinful man!" (Luke 5:8), we must all admit we are sinners and then acknowledge that Jesus is the Son of God. Jesus replies to the heart of such a sincere prayer with, "Don't be afraid. Follow me!" If you are ready to take this first step of faith, please turn to page 34 to pray this prayer of commitment. It will also aid you in following Jesus in your new walk of faith.

We are going to travel down the road a little further today with Jesus and His new followers. Jesus wasn't about to let their new-found faith die for lack of excitement. He knew that bored anglers would result in boring disciples. He needed these men to spread the gospel with excitement and anticipation.

Have you ever considered Christianity boring? Why?

_____

_____

Rate the following activities from 1 to 10 with 1 being the most exciting and 10 so boring you could sleep.

_____Sports events   _____Bible study
_____Religious activities   _____Shopping
_____Vacations   _____Cleaning the house
_____Prayer   _____Emailing friends
_____Paying Bills   _____Church services

Okay, I admit I have attended a few boring church services, church meetings, and prayer groups. A few of them would even rank lower than paying bills in yawn-producing activities. However, when I search the Bible, I do not see Jesus boring the people around Him.

Let's move down the road to Galilee with Jesus and His new disciples. Read the following passages and note the people's reaction to Jesus, His Words, and His actions.

Read John 1:35-50. List all the men who are now with Jesus in His travels:

_____

_____

In this passage, we read that Andrew, Simon Peter, John, Philip, and Nathaniel are now following Jesus. For fun, let's add our own name to this list. Let's imagine ourselves as participating in the next event in faith motivation.

Read John 2:1-11. Who was at the wedding with Jesus?

_____

_____

What miracle did Jesus perform?

_____

How did the wine compare to the wine already consumed?

_____

What reaction did the disciples have in verse 11?

_____

_____

Jesus, His mother, and His new followers attended the wedding in Cana. To the concern of Mary, the host had run out of wine to serve his guests. In the ancient Jewish culture, this problem would have caused great humiliation to the groom and his family. So, at His mother's urging, Jesus turned the water

Faith Fact
In the beginning, Jesus might use fun and the spectacular to thrill our faith to fruition.

into magnificent wine. In your opinion, why do you think Jesus performed this miracle?

_____

_____

Certainly, Jesus' compassion influenced His decision that the party could continue in a joyous celebration. He honored Mary by fulfilling her request. However, I believe He wanted to wow His new followers. Verse 11 states that He thus revealed His glory and His disciples put their faith in Him. The phrase "put their faith" translates from the original Greek word, *pisteúō*. *Pisteúō* has a broader definition that helps us gain a clearer idea why the disciples' faith increased. It conveys the idea of "to be firmly persuaded as to something, to believe whole heartedly. To believe in God, to trust Him as able and willing to help and answer prayer." [2]

One of my first experiences as a new believer occurred not at a wedding, but on a lakeshore. Our church's youth group drove five hours to swim at a popular lake resort. The harried youth pastor had placed the keys to the church van in the pocket of his swim trunks. Oops! You guessed it. The keys floated out unnoticed until the group of hot, tired, and now-hungry teenagers wanted to go get something to eat. Our weary pastor reached for the keys—no keys. Tempers flared and the group of cranky teens broke into accusations. Suddenly, one of the younger girls, said, "Let's pray!" We joined hands and said a halfhearted prayer to find the ring of keys.

Most of us began to search the beach; however, the younger girl started to wade into the waves of the lake. About ten steps out she felt something hard and sharp underneath her bare foot. God displayed His ability to hear our doubting words and produced the set of keys. I believe He did this out of compassion for our pastor, but also to increase our faith. It did mine; I will never forget the feeling of astonishment.

Now it's your turn. Can you recall when Christ did something spectacular that increased your faith? If yes, describe the circumstance and then jot down how you felt at the time.

_____

Sit still for a few minutes. Ponder the activities of Jesus in your life. Then write a prayer asking Him to increase your faith in a new and amazing way.

Lord Jesus,

In Your name, Amen

Faith Finale!

This, the first of His miraculous signs, Jesus performed at Cana in Galilee. He thus revealed His glory, and His disciples put their faith in Him. John 2:11

Day 3 – **Itsy Bitsy Faith**

Lord,

At times my faith can be miniscule. As I begin today's lesson, cultivate my faith. Help my faith to grow strong and sturdy.

In Your name, Amen.

The icy roads threatened accidents. My friend and I proceeded cautiously down the slick hill. Suddenly, we began to slide. Unable to control the Volkswagen Beetle, we headed in the direction of a huge red luxury sedan. I was a new believer to the Christian faith. I had no training in the subject of prayer and faith. All I thought to do was say, "Jesus, Jesus!"

Faith Fun

If you have ever fallen asleep in a church service or a church meeting, you are not alone. Read Acts 20:7-12. Now, the moral to this story is, don't sit in a warm room on a window ledge if the meeting is going to drag on all night.

The car continued to skid toward the ruby monster. We braced ourselves for impact when our tiny car halted. Shocked, I looked at my friend. Her mouth agape, she stared back. We opened the doors cautiously and stepped gingerly on the ice. We crept forward toward the front bumper of our vehicle. We discovered we could not have slid a piece of paper between the two cars, but we didn't smash into the sedan. This event became another faith seed. God had heard my squeaky voice and answered swiftly. My itsy-bitsy faith grew a little that day.

Contrary to popular belief, God doesn't expect us to start out as giants of faith. Of course, that would be great, but it just doesn't work that way. Throughout Scripture, we see people who struggled to place trust in an unseen God. Yet, repeatedly God transformed these ordinary individuals into what we now call "heroes of faith." This cultivation of faith is a lifetime process.

Faith Fiction
Great faith is an automatic component of a believer's walk.

Please read Luke 17:3-5. What did the disciples request of Jesus?

_____

What command of Jesus prompted this request?

_____

Jesus utilized the difficult issue of an unforgiving heart to help the disciples recognize their lack of faith. Forgiving someone who has hurt us deeply can seem impossible. As women, we face times we may have to forgive someone for a betrayal, an abuse, or just annoyances. The list could go on with endless probabilities of offenses we are called to forgive. Any situation where forgiveness is needed requires a concentrated effort on our part, doesn't it?

However, Jesus doesn't stop with asking the disciples to forgive once. He tells them to forgive as many times as needed. I don't know about you, but to *keep* forgiving someone for a repeated offense is hard! Can you imagine the thoughts of these disciples as they looked at each other with disbelief on their faces? They were Jewish men who only knew the Law of Moses. It contained hard and fast rules for retribution. For example, "If anyone injures his neighbor, whatever he has done must be done to him: fracture for fracture, eye for eye, tooth for tooth. As he has injured the other, so he is to be injured" (Leviticus 24:19, 20). Now Jesus instructs them to forgive and then forgive again. I imagine an image of someone they held a grudge against flitted within their minds. Now that is a faith shaker!

Or perhaps, they were simply annoyed with someone for a continuing behavior. I annoy my husband by leaving coffee cups around the house. I may set one on a closet shelf, forget where I placed it, and go for a fresh cup. Within a few minutes, I may leave that cup sitting in the garage. Guess who ends up finding the missing java? My husband. He has asked me repeatedly not to travel around the house depositing my mugs because they attract ants. After more than twenty years of marriage, cold stale coffee cups still greet him on a regular basis. Now he just picks them up, places them in the dishwasher and grabs the bug spray. He has learned the art of forgiving an annoying behavior.

I think most of us can relate to people who continue to annoy us or to the bitterness of unforgiveness. Jesus says, ""Forgive him" (Luke 17-4b). That requires a lot of faith—faith that God is big enough and wise enough to handle the person or situation without our negativity or input.

Now place yourself in the disciples' sandals for a moment. Why do you think they said, "Increase our faith!"? (Luke 17:5). Doesn't it make you smile to imagine the look on their faces as they pleaded for faith?

_____

_____

Read Luke 17:6. How did He respond?

_____

The disciples asked for their faith to be increased. Jesus responded to them with the concept that even if their faith was as small as a mustard seed it could uproot a huge mulberry bush. In ancient times, the mustard seed was known to be one of the smallest types of seeds. It is only mentioned in the New Testament and each instance it is referenced as something tiny. Although there were smaller seeds, the mustard seed was used as a common analogy for smallness. Ancient Jewish teachers often used the phrase "grain of mustard" when referring to something miniscule. This phrase was as common to the Jewish people as it is for us to say, "Hey, just email me."

Here's a little background information for this word picture. The itsy-bitsy mustard seed actually grows into a bush, not a tree. However, in ancient Palestine,

21

those bushes grew to the height of 12 to 15 feet. They were large enough for birds to perch in the branches. In contrast, the mulberry tree's roots grew deep and wide. It seemed an impossibility to move it with any type of tool, let alone a kernel of faith.

Jesus and the disciples realized how difficult it was to forgive someone who hurts us deeply or annoys us with the same irritating behaviors. Harsh attitudes toward other people can resemble a deeply rooted tree in our lives. It's hard to dig it out once it begins to take root.

How do you think mustard seed faith could help us to forgive?

_____

_____

If I possess just a tiny bit of faith, I can rely on God to do the rest which is an encouragement to me. I may have to forgive and forgive and forgive, but with God's help, I can accomplish the seemingly impossible task of repeated forgiveness. Oh Lord, "Increase my faith!"

Christ gave another example of mustard seed faith to His disciples. Read Matthew 17:14-20.

What was the problem?

_____

Who tried to resolve the issue?

_____

What was the outcome?

_____

What did the disciples ask Jesus?

_____

What was Christ's response?

_____

The disciples could not cure the young man. The father said, "I brought him to your disciples, but they could not heal him" (Matthew 17:16). Jesus quickly rebuked the demon and the boy was healed from that moment. Once again, I smile at the disciples.

How did the disciples come to Jesus?

_____

_____

They came in private. That's what I would have done too. I don't know about you, but when my faith is shaky, I do not want to parade it in front of others. The disciples had already been embarrassed by their lack of healing ability; I doubt they wanted the world to hear what the problem was with the whole episode. I would have slunk out of the crowd and waited to get Jesus by Himself to ask, "Hey, why couldn't I do that?"

Mark an X on the line below to indicate what type of faith you have at the moment.

_____

Zero   Smaller than a mustard seed   A mustard seed   A new budding plant   A giant tree

Our faith can vary according to circumstances. In some areas we can have great faith and in others doubt may overwhelm us. Answer the following questions to help yourself identify your weak and strong areas of faith.

In what areas do you have strong faith?

_____

_____

Why is your faith strong in these areas?

_____

_____

In what areas is your faith like an itsy-bitsy mustard seed?

_____

_____

What type of mountain needs to move in your life?

_____

_____

He said to them, "Because of the littleness of your faith [that is, your lack of firmly relying trust]. For truly I say to you, if you have faith [that is living] like a grain of mustard seed, you can say to this mountain, Move from here to yonder place, and it will move; and nothing will be impossible to you."

Matthew 17:20, AMP

Do you believe it is possible to move? Why or why not?

_____

_____

We all have areas where our faith is weaker than in other areas. No matter how strong or weak our faith, God desires for it to increase. Jesus didn't chide the men for asking, "Why couldn't we drive it out?" Please read Jesus' response in the Amplified Bible found in the margin.

This explains it was actually not their "littleness" of faith, but their lack of firmly trusting God for the results. Their faith was flawed because they doubted. Jesus implied their faith was dead, not living. But if they had living faith as small as a mustard seed they could tell the mountain to move and it would move. Nothing would be impossible if their faith was alive and planted in God.

Faith Fact
Increased faith comes by hearing and studying the Word of God.

Jesus desires that we live faith-filled lives. He strives to make our faith grow. Let's find out the primary way we can grow our faith. Read Romans 10:17 and then paraphrase this verse.

_____

_____

Let's be encouraged by the fact that our faith will increase as we study God's Word. In closing today, contemplate our "Faith Finale" verse. Then let's take a moment to write a prayer and ask Jesus to "increase our faith."

Faith Finale!

I tell you the truth, if you have faith as small as a mustard seed, you can say to this mountain, "Move from here to there" and it will move. Nothing will be impossible for you. Matthew 17:20

Lord Jesus,

In Your name, Amen

Day 4 – **Stained Glass Saints**

Father,

I often compare my faith to other people's faith. I always seem to come up short in comparison. Today teach me that my faith is individual. Help me to believe that You will grow my mustard seed faith in Your perfect timing and Your perfect way.

In Jesus' name, Amen

I strolled through an old church cemetery with graves dating back to the 1200s. Although the headstones were weather beaten and worn, I could still read a few of the inscriptions.

> She walked with God.
> He lived faithful.
> Rest as You Lived, in God's Peace

Faith Fun

List your own annoying bad habits that you are currently working on to overcome. Next to each habit list the people who need an increase of faith to keep their patience with you while you break the bad habits for good.

1. _____

2. _____

3. _____

4. _____

5. _____

25

I gazed at the stone church. The evening sun danced off the stained glass windows. I studied the pious and serene expressions on saints' faces silhouetted within the windows. I wondered to myself, "Did any of these people experience a shrinking of their faith?" My own inadequate faith seems to expand and deflate with various life experiences.

Perhaps you feel the same way I do? Does your faith waver? Do you feel at times that your faith might be shrinking instead of growing? If you answered yes, I say, "Welcome to the crowd!" In today's lesson, we are going to study the followers of Jesus and their thoughts about trusting God. We saw they asked, "Increase our faith!" We examined how Jesus used the spectacular to sprout the disciples' faith in the beginning of their walk with Him. Today, we'll research the stability of their new-found faith. Read Matthew 14:22-33. In verses 22-26, where were the disciples? Where was Christ?

_____

_____

What did Jesus say in response to their terror?

_____

What challenge did Peter put forth?

_____

Describe how Peter's faith faltered.

_____

_____

How did Jesus respond to Peter's drowning faith?

_____

At His command, the disciples set off in the boat without Jesus. As they struggled with the boat because of the high winds, they looked up to see what appeared to be an apparition walking on the water. Good news for them—it was Jesus!

Peter's faith surges and he wants to join Jesus atop the waves. However, after he hops out of the boat, he takes his eyes off the Lord. His faith falters, resulting in his physical body sinking. I think Jesus probably said the following words with a tender smile, "You of little faith, why did you doubt?" (Matthew 14:30-32).

Please reread verses 32, 33. What was the result of the disciples' scare and their shaken faith?

_____

Their faith increased! These verses say they worshiped Him and said, "Truly you are the Son of God" (Matthew 14:33). Now recall that they had seen miracles before this episode, yet when fear struck, doubt arose. But even though their faith shrank for a short time, their faith grew stronger through the incident.

Let's peek at two more episodes where our serene, stained-glass saints reacted with shattered doubt. Please read Mark 6:30-44.

According to verse 34, what emotion did Jesus possess for the crowd?

_____

What was the disciples' concern in verses 35, 36?

_____

What do you think spurred their concern—compassion or their own hunger? (verse 31)

_____

What was Jesus' response?

_____

_____

What do you think went through their minds?

_____

_____

Faith Fiction
Real faith is unshakeable. It remains strong throughout any circumstance.

27

How many people do you think fives loaves of bread and two fish would have fed if Jesus had not intervened?

_____

What did Jesus do?

_____

What was the result according to verse 42?

_____

Jesus had compassion for the multitude of people who sought Him out. The disciples might have been concerned for the crowds' welfare, also. However, I think their own stomachs were growling and they wanted to eat.

Jesus satisfied their hunger both spiritually and physically. However, the guys still didn't understand the whole picture. Now continue to read Mark 6:45-52. This is the same story we read earlier in Matthew about Jesus walking on the water. What does verse 52 state about the disciples' understanding of Jesus feeding the five thousand?

These guys just didn't get it. They were fed and that was that. So, they needed to repeat the lunchtime lesson. Read Mark 8:1-10. Write down all the similarities between the two different occasions of Jesus feeding the multitudes.

Did you find that Jesus had compassion for the people? His compassion reached out not only to the crowds, but also to His twelve followers. Christ wanted them to understand that He could provide for their needs. Therefore, He went through the whole routine again for their sakes.
- He asked, "How many loaves do you have?" (Mark 6:38 and 8:5)
- He gave thanks to the Father for the food.
- He distributed it until everyone was satisfied.
- The disciples gathered the leftovers in baskets.

In Mark 6:42, 43 it is interesting to note that the disciples collected 12 baskets of leftovers. They each had "to-go" for their next meal. In Mark 8:8, the retrieved baskets were numbered at seven. Throughout the Bible, the number seven is considered to represent the idea of completion and perfection. Perhaps, the disciples had completed and passed their lesson in this area of their faith. Okay, now here is the real kicker. Finish reading Mark 8:14-21. What questions did Jesus ask His dull-in-faith friends?

What was the final question that He asked in verse 21?
In today's vernacular, Jesus was saying "Duh! Don't you get it yet?"

Describe a time when God repeated a lesson in your life.

_____

_____

What area of faith could you use a refresher course in right now?

_____

Well, as you can see, the 12 closest friends of Jesus didn't always live up to the faith-filled images we see in stained glass church windows. They struggled with doubt and dullness of heart. They certainly had many "duh moments" in their relationship with the Son of God.

Today, I hope you are encouraged by the disciples' ineptitude of grasping at their faith lesson. They didn't get it right much of the time. What can we learn from them in today's lesson? Let's give ourselves a little slack in this journey of faith. Yes, our mustard seed faith might sprout up, but it might wilt too. If it does, Jesus will reach out His hand to lift us back to walk a life of faith. And you might hear Him say, "My daughter, why did you doubt?"

As we pray today, let's ask Him if we need any repeat faith lessons. Then take a few moments, to thank Jesus for His patience with us faith-fractured saints.

Sweet Jesus,

Faith Fun

Pretend it's 500 years from today. Someone is reading your epitaph on a marble tombstone. What would it say about your faith today? What do you hope it *will* say about the faith you lived?

In Your name, Amen

Faith Finale!

Immediately Jesus reached out his hand and caught him. "You of little faith," he said, "why did you doubt?" And when they climbed into the boat, the wind died down. Then those who were in the boat worshiped him, saying, "Truly you are the Son of God." Matthew 14:31-33

Day 5 – **Old Faithful**

Father,

Today as I study Your Word, allow the truth of Your faithfulness to penetrate my heart. Help me to understand that Your faithfulness is never-ending in my life, regardless of what my feelings tell me.

In Jesus' name, Amen

We waited and waited. Then finally, I stood in awe as the geyser, Old Faithful, spewed steaming water 150 feet into the air. The Yellowstone National Park ranger told us that it was myth that the geyser shot into the air every ninety-six minutes. He said it is faithful to spray the water, but not on man's timetable. Doesn't that sound like God? Scripture repeatedly states that God is faithful beyond our imagination. However, sometimes we doubt. The problem is that we

30

want Him to act in faithfulness according to our requests, standards, and time schedules. We especially feel that way when problems rattle our lives. We ask, "Where is the faithfulness of God *right* now?"

As we close out this week's lesson, we will research the Scriptures that assure us of God's faithfulness when those moments of doubt threaten to dissolve our trust. They will be our foundation over the next five weeks as we learn more about growing our faith.

Please read the following Scriptures and then note what they state about God's faithfulness: Psalm 36:5, 89:8, 91:4, 100:5.

God's faithfulness continues through all generations and it reaches to the skies. His faithfulness surrounds Him and protects us as a shield. Why? Why *is* God so faithful to us? Let's find out the reason. Please fill-in the missing words in each of the following verses.

But you, O Lord, are a compassionate and gracious God, slow to anger, abounding in _____ and _____. Psalm 86:15

I will sing of the Lord's great _____ forever; with my mouth I will make your _____ known through all generations. I will declare that your _____stands firm forever, that you established your _____ in heaven itself. Psalm 89:1-2

For great is your _____, higher than the heavens; your _____ reaches to the skies. Psalm 108:4

For great is his_____toward us, and the_ _____of the Lord endures forever. Psalm 117:2

Do you believe that Jesus loves *you*? Why or why not?

_____

_____

Please read John 3:16 and Romans 5:8. How do they prove to you that God loves you? In the margin, will you please insert your name in the blanks of these paraphrased verses?

_____

_____

The Lord God loves us. He gave us Jesus as proof of that love. It goes back to the old childhood song "Jesus Loves Me."

> Jesus loves me. This I know,
> for the Bible tells me so.
> Little ones to Him belong:
> For they are weak and He is strong.
> Yes, Jesus loves me!
> Yes, Jesus loves me!
> Yes, Jesus loves me!
> The Bible tells me so.[3]

Faith Fact
God is faithful to us because He loves us.

Jesus loves us, but that doesn't translate to Him responding in faithfulness to our time schedule. The geyser, Old Faithful, demonstrates this truth to us. The park guide explained that after the earthquakes in 1959, 1983, and 1998, the average length between the geyser's eruptions increased. Where it once was about 76 minutes, it is now approximately 90 minutes between eruptions. Just like Old Faithful, I have found that as God increases my faith, He sometimes increases the time between my "earthquake" and His rescue. If and when a longer time span does occur between crisis and aid, it allows me to anticipate and depend upon His yet unseen faithfulness.

Let's read a story in which Jesus purposely delayed His coming so people's faith might be increased. Read John 11:1-45. According to verse 5, how did Jesus feel about Martha and Mary? How long did He delay?

_____

_____

Why did He delay according to verse 14?

_____

What emotion did Jesus demonstrate in verses 34-36?

_____

What question did the naysayers ask?

_____

What was the result of Lazarus being raised from the dead in verse 45?

_____

Martha and Mary wanted the Lord to react like a genie in a bottle. Many times, so do we. We call out our wishes and we demand He bring about miraculous results. I recently witnessed this attitude in an unbelieving friend. Unexpectedly, she landed in the hospital with an undiagnosed problem. Frustrated, she said, "I cried out to God last night and He didn't heal me! What kind of God is He?" Although my friend never gave a thought about God until a crisis arose, she expected His immediate help when she called out. She demanded the Lord be faithful to her needs on her schedule. Her disappointment resulted in a defiant attitude of doubt much like Martha and Mary experienced in the beginning of their ordeal with Lazarus' death.

Earthquakes of trouble may rattle our lives. We may feel He delays, but God's faithfulness does not depend upon our expectations. In closing today, write a prayer to Christ based on the verses of Psalm 46 found in the margin.

I pray that this lesson has helped each of us to understand that God loves us and He is always faithful. There is a popular saying, "God is rarely early, but He is never late." He will always prove faithful. Next week we are going to study how God strengthens our sprouted faith by asking us to step out from the dark and to trust His light.

Faith Finale!
For great is his love toward us, and the faithfulness of the Lord endures forever. Praise the LORD. Psalm 117:2

Faith Fiction
God reacts in faithfulness on our time schedule.

God is our refuge and strength, an ever-present help in trouble. Therefore, we will not fear, though the earth give way and the mountains fall into the heart of the sea though its waters roar and foam and the mountains quake with their surging ...Be still, and know that I am God; I will be exalted among the nations, I will be exalted in the earth.
Psalm 46:1-3, 10

Faith Fun
Dig out a cookbook or look online at a recipe for bagels. What are all the different cooking methods and lengths of time it takes before a bagel is ready to devour? How could a bagel demonstrate God building our faith?

Faith Seed Thoughts & Prayers – **Review Week 1**

Journal your thoughts about how this week's lessons applied to you personally.

Prayer of Salvation

Lord Jesus,

I am reaching out in faith to You. I believe that You are the Son of the Living God. I am a sinner. I confess my sin to You and believe that by Your death and resurrection You forgive me. Help me to grow in my new faith. Teach me how to allow You to be the Lord of my life.

I pray this in Your name, Amen

1 Dean, Jennifer Kennedy. Fueled by Faith (Birmingham, AL: New Hope Publishers, 2005), pp.155, 156.

2 Zodhiates, Spiros. Th.D., The Complete Word Study Dictionary: New Testament. AMG Publishers, Chattanooga, TN. 1992. P. 1160-1161 #4100.

3 Warner, Annna B. 1860.

Week 2
Scared of the Dark

Day 1 – **I'm Scared!**

Dear God,

Sometimes it's scary to step out in faith. Grant me the nerve to walk in the areas where my faith is shaky. Help me to take the first little step outside my comfort zone.

In Your Son's name, Amen

Five-year-old Johnny was in the kitchen as his mother made supper. She asked him to go into the pantry and get her a can of tomato soup, but he didn't want to go in alone. "It's dark in there and I'm scared," he said. She asked again, but he persisted. Finally, she said, "It's Okay—Jesus will be in there with you." Johnny walked hesitantly to the door and slowly opened it. He peeked inside and saw it was dark. Johnny started to leave, when all at once an idea came to mind. He asked, "Jesus, if You're in there, would You hand me a can of tomato soup?"

Have you ever felt like Johnny? I have. At times, stepping out in faith is scary. Even when we know God is there for us, it still feels like we are jumping into a void and falling fast.

Fortunately, God acknowledges our fears, and He realizes we need encouragement, not condemnation. So, for those reasons, He recorded in the

Bible numerous stories of men and women who were frightened, but made the leap into faith. These accounts not only reveal the fear of the individuals, but also the benefits of overcoming the terror and learning to trust God.

This week we will focus on several "fraidy-cats" who became legendary lions amid trembling faith. Let's illuminate the frightful darkness of our fear with some light from God's Word. Read Exodus 3:1-6 and then answer the following questions. What did Moses do when he saw the strange sight of the bush on fire?

_____

Stand in Moses' sandals for a moment. Describe what you would do.

_____

What did God say to Moses?

_____

What emotion did Moses experience in verse 6?

_____

And God said, "I will be with you." Exodus 3:12a

Moses spotted something intriguing during an ordinary day of tending sheep. He decided to take a closer look and suddenly heard God speak. Scared to look any closer, Moses hid his face.

Do you relate to Moses? I do. I want to see and hear God in my life. Yet, when it starts to happen, I back away—afraid. I'm afraid, because I am unsure of God and because I am uncertain of myself. Fear is often based on the unknown. Let's read a few more verses to see how this fear of the unknown played out between God and Moses.

Read Exodus 3:7-15, 4:1-5. Note in the following verses who Moses felt unsure about—God or himself. Jot down God's response to Moses' uncertainty.

Verses 3:11,12 _____

Verses 3:13,14 _____

Verses 4:1-5 _____

It often happens that as I read my Bible, I feel inspired to act for God. Just like Moses, I pray, "Here I am." But then, I get my marching orders from God—and YIKES! I am either scared or just don't want to complete *that* assignment. Can you describe a time when you were scared to do what you felt God was asking of you? Or, was there a time you just did not want to do what God requested? Why?

_____

_____

How did your faith play a part in your response?

_____

Let's not forget that Moses was speaking with God from a burning bush. It seems this experience would create an enormous amount of faith, doesn't it? Yet, Moses wallowed in doubt of both God's ability and his own. Moses wasn't about to step into the position of leading the Israelites out of captivity without an argument. Read Exodus 4:10-12. What was Moses' excuse?

_____

How did the Lord respond in verse 10?

_____

Write down the Lord's reply in verse 12.

_____

Did you know public speaking is one of the top fears among people? Many people feel nauseous, sweaty, and shaky when they speak before an audience. A few speakers faint from fear. Author and speaker, John Ortberg, writes of this embarrassing experience.

> One Sunday early on, I was about ten minutes into the message when I started getting very warm and dizzy. The next thing I knew . . . I had fainted in the middle of a sermon. The very next time I went to preach, the same thing happened. I went down ten minutes into the talk . . . Well-meaning people offered all kinds of advice: "You just need to try really hard to relax and trust more" . . . I asked God to take away the fear of it happening again. He didn't.[1]

It seems Moses held this phobia too. Forget the movie version with the eloquent Charleton Heston. Oh no, the real Moses was slow in speech and tongue, and he knew it.

However, that didn't deter God. He basically said, "Hey, I know how you speak. I gave you your mouth and speech. Now go!"

Mark on the scale below your feelings about speaking in public.

_____

No way   Nauseated   Stuttering   Sweaty palms & butterflies   Where's the microphone?

Moses peered into the dark fear of speaking to Pharaoh and his faith faltered. "No way," he thought. In a last ditch effort, he pleaded with God. Write what Moses said in Exodus 4:13.

_____

_____

What final answer did the Lord give to Moses? (verses 14-17)

_____

As we close today's lesson, I want us to ponder two final verses. Read the following verses and then underline any phrases that might encourage an increase in your faith. Then, note your thoughts about Moses and his lack of faith in God's ability to equip him.

_____

_____

For God did not give us a spirit of timidity, but a spirit of power, of love and of self-discipline. 2 Timothy 1:7

Moses was educated in all the wisdom of the Egyptians and was powerful in speech and action. Acts 7:22

Moses behaved like the little boy Johnny who was afraid to go into the pantry for soup. Even though God was going to be with both Moses and Johnny, their fear and lack of faith in God's presence hindered them. However, in the case of Moses, the Lord proved more than faithful as we read in Acts 7:22.

So how about you? Is there something hidden deep in your dark pantry of faith that needs to be pulled out? Let's ask the Lord to illuminate His ability to give us the spirit of power when we are frightened by our lack of faith in God and ourselves.

Lord God,

In Jesus' name, Amen

Faith Fact
The Lord will equip those He calls to act.

Faith Fun
If God asked you to do the following, how would you respond?
- Ask my cranky mother-in-law over for dinner
- Say "yes" to leading a women's small group
- Plan a romantic get-away with my husband
- Speak to an arena of people
- Give additional money to my church
- Pray aloud in a group
- Invite my co-worker to church
- Watch the neighbor's rambunctious kids

Faith Finale!
For God did not give us a spirit of timidity, but a spirit of power, of love and of self-discipline. 2 Timothy 1:7

Day 2 – **Fraidy-Cats**

Jesus,

I lack courage. Sometimes I am afraid to act in faith. Lord, remind me that I can trust You to never leave me nor forsake me, and that You will always be by my side. Help me not to be afraid.

                                                            In Your name, I pray, Amen.

"Somebody pulled my tail," says the Cowardly Lion in the *Wizard of Oz*. The brainless Scarecrow astutely points out that the Cowardly Lion is twisting it between his own hands. Duh! The big brawny lion was a fraidy-cat at heart. He longed for courage, but sorely lacked the self-esteem to acquire it without the help of his friends and, of course, the legendary Wizard of Oz.

The Cowardly Lion felt shame because he knew he should be the courageous king of the forest. Yet, fear paralyzed his potential. I can relate to the Cowardly Lion. As a child of God, I know intellectually He will look after me. Yet in my heart, I feel all alone and tremble at the thought of walking in faith in areas that frighten me.

In today's lesson, we will study the issue of being a fraidy-cat and how God responds to our fear. Okay, let's quit twisting our tails and learn why we can be courageous in our faith. Read Joshua 1:5-9. What promise is stated in both verses 5 and 9?

_____

What repeated commands do we find in verses 6, 7, and 9?

_____

Because God repeated to Joshua, "Be strong and courageous," three times within five verses, what would you assume Joshua must have been feeling?

_____

Describe how the promise "I will never leave you or forsake you" should set the foundation for the command, "Be strong and very courageous."

_____

Describe a time when life wasn't going as you planned it.

_____

_____

Faith Fiction
God expects us never to be afraid.

Did you feel fear? If yes, why?

_____

Did anyone say something similar to "Have faith—God is in complete control."? How did that make you feel?

_____

_____

For myself, when I am scared about a circumstance in life, I feel frustrated when someone encourages me to "just have faith." Easier said than done! However, I have discovered a remedy for those times when I feel like a fraidy-cat. I repeat God's promise that He will never leave me. It calms and steadies me. God's promise helps me to be stronger when life shakes me up.

This assurance of God's presence is given throughout Scripture. Let's examine a few of these passages. Match the verse reference with the correct phrase.

Deuteronomy 31:8   "And surely I am with you always,
                         to the very end of the age."

Isaiah 41:10a   "The Lord himself goes before you and will be with
                         you; he will never leave you nor forsake you."

Matthew 28:20b   "So do not fear, for I am with you;
                         do not be dismayed, for I am your God."

Read Hebrews 13:5b-6a in the margin.

For He [God] Himself has said, I will not in any way fail you nor give you up nor leave you without support. [I will] not, [I will] not, [I will] not in any degree leave you helpless nor forsake nor let [you] down (relax My hold on you)! [Assuredly not!] So we take comfort and are encouraged and confidently and boldly say, The Lord is my Helper; I will not be seized with alarm [I will not fear or dread or be terrified]. What can man do to me?
Hebrews 13:5b-6a, AMP

How does this apply to Joshua?

_____

Do you believe it for yourself? Why or why not?

_____

Faith Fact
God is always with us.

My friend, let's memorize Joshua 1:9. As we memorize it, let's place our own name within the verse.

_____, *be strong and courageous. Do not be terrified; do not be*
      Your Name

discouraged, for the Lord my God will be with me wherever I go.

God understands that we may experience fear when things are out of control. Read our final passage to discover how Jesus tames our fears: Mark 4:35-41. Consider this scene of the disciples on the boat, in conjunction with what the Lord told Joshua. "Be strong and courageous. Do not be terrified; do not be discouraged for the Lord your God goes with you wherever you go" (Joshua 1:9). These words would have been very familiar to the Jewish disciples. Now let's envision ourselves as the disciples in the boat.

What caused our initial fear?

_____

Remembering the assurance given to Joshua, what tone of voice did you imagine that might have Jesus used when He asked us, "Why are you so afraid? Do you still have no faith?"

_____

In verse 41, why were they terrified? What type of expression crossed Jesus' face as we asked each other, "Who is this?"

_____

For me, anxiety would have wracked my entire being. I would have pounded on Jesus to wake up and help with bailing out the water. However, to my surprise, Jesus didn't grab a bucket. Instead, He calmed the storm with just three words. "Quiet! Be still" (verse 39).
So what about us? Why *are* we such fraidy-cats when it comes to trusting that Jesus will be with us always? Let's confess our fear and ask Him to remind us to be strong and courageous in our faith.

Jesus,

In Your powerful name, Amen

Faith Finale!

Do not be afraid or terrified because of them, for the LORD your God goes with you; he will never leave you nor forsake you.   Deuteronomy 31:6

Day 3 – **Second Guessing**

Father,

Sometimes I doubt what I am supposed to do. Please be patient with me when I second-guess Your directions in my life. Allow me to see Your will and step out in faith.

In Jesus' name, Amen.

A few years ago, I felt God nudge me to invite my neighbor to join my home Bible study group. I had no inkling if the woman even believed in a god, let alone Jesus Christ. I chose to ignore His instruction to me. The group began on a Tuesday—without my neighbor. By Thursday, I felt guilty. I prayed about it. Once again, I felt I should ask her. "Okay, Lord, I need You to prove that You want me to do this." Coincidentally, the mail carrier mistakenly delivered her mail to my house that afternoon!

Faith Fun
Unscramble the words for some of our most common fears.

diserps

gusb

dolsecne

caspes

ehisthg

ehadt

llssien

I trudged across the street and reluctantly knocked on her door. I second-guessed my decision to approach her. She answered the door with a slightly surprised look on her face. I handed her the mail. My voice squeaked, "You wouldn't want to come to a Bible study that I hold at my home on Tuesday, would you?" I expected a complete and absolute rejection. To my surprise she answered, "I would love to come. What time?"

Later, I discovered she battled a chronic liver condition. She needed not only the support of friends, but she needed the Lord to come and renew the faith that had begun in her as a child. I didn't know all those details, but God did.
Let's examine another person who was afraid to act when God spoke. Read Judges 6:6, 11-18.

Why was Gideon threshing wheat in a winepress?

_____

What familiar phrase pops up again in verse 12?

_____

By what name did the Lord address Gideon?

_____

Because of the oppression of the Midianites, Gideon hid in a winepress to thresh wheat. Suddenly, the Lord appeared and spoke to Gideon. Once again, we see the familiar phrase, "The Lord is with you." (The Lord can find us even when we hide.) Then the Lord addressed fraidy-cat Gideon as "mighty warrior." It seems the Lord knew something about Gideon that he didn't recognize in himself. He was a warrior for God. I would have loved to have seen his face when he heard, "The Lord is with you, mighty warrior."

Regardless of what he thought, Gideon asked God some honest questions. Read Judges 6:13-16.

Write the first question he asked God.

_____

Can you describe a time when you felt like asking God, "Why?"

_____

Did the Lord answer Gideon's question?

_____

Did He answer yours?

_____

Usually, we do not get a direct answer to our "whys." Instead, God desires that we trust Him with the outcome. In this instance, the Lord wanted Gideon to walk in faith as a mighty warrior as part of the answers to the questions. However, Gideon, not unlike Moses, responded with a few excuses. "My clan is the weakest in Manasseh, and I am the least in my family" (verse 15b).

How about you? List excuses you have given God when you preferred to hide rather than act?

1. _____

2. _____

3. _____

God told Gideon, "Go in the strength you have" (verse 14). List three strengths that might help you in following God's divine will (health, money, talent, education, etc.). I have added two additional strengths that apply to each of us.

1. _____

2. _____

3. _____

4. God is sending us. (verse 14) _____

5. He will be with us. (verse 16) _____

Faith Fiction
God is always angry when we doubt and ask again.

45

Read Judges 6:17-18. The following is one of my favorite passages of Scripture. I sense the doubt and insecurity of Gideon when he says in today's vernacular, "Give me a sign that it is really You talking to me." I have prayed those same words many times. Although the Lord would prefer our faith to be unshakable, I do not think He minds reassuring us. I feel He responds in tender understanding to Gideon's shaky faith. The Lord promises, "I will wait until you return." Don't you love that? Can you visualize Gideon scrambling to get the offering prepared? I wonder what thoughts raced through his mind. What would you have been thinking?

Gideon brought his offering to God and then received his marching orders to free the Israelites from their enemies. As the story progresses, Gideon still doubts what he heard from God.

Read Judges 6:36-39. What does Gideon ask God to perform in order to assure him he has heard correctly?

_____

Wet. No, now I want it dry! This is the famous story of the fleece. We often talk about or hear the phrase, "I set out a fleece." Gideon started the whole process of "putting out a fleece" to confirm a decision he was unsure about.

Have you ever "set out a fleece"? If yes, what were the circumstances? Did the "fleece" help you make the decision?

_____

_____

A few years ago, my church decided to start a church plant across town. I volunteered to lead a Bible study at the fledgling church. However, before I knew it, the senior pastor appointed me as the women's ministries director. I could feel the fear and inadequacy rise in my heart every time I thought about it. One evening at our Wednesday night service I prayed, "Lord, confirm to me if I am supposed to take this position. I don't feel I have the abilities to take on such a role." To my shock, within fifteen minutes, my face appeared on the giant video monitor in my home church with the caption announcing, "Susanne Scheppmann—Women's Ministries Director in our new church." I knew it was the answer to my "fleece."

Let's peek at a couple of other biblical examples of people who felt they needed a second confirmation of direction. Read 1 Samuel 23:1-5.

What caused David to double check with the Lord concerning fighting against the Philistines?

_____

His men questioned the decision. David had enough sense to listen to them and then to pray again for guidance before launching the assault. I believe it is important to seek counsel and advice before making decisions. Listen to what others have to say, and then seek the Lord again for final direction. God did not chide David for seeking confirmation on whether to proceed with his original choice.

Below check the people whom you might seek out for counsel when making a decision.

    ____ Pastor   ____ employer

    ____ husband   ____ in-law

    ____ friend   ____ sister/brother

    ____ mother   ____ church leader

    ____ father   ____ other

If the counsel went against the original decision, what would you do?

_____

If you prayed and felt the Lord confirmed your initial choice, would you proceed? If yes, how difficult would it be?

_____

I don't know about you, but I can be very indecisive. I used to prefer that other people make the decisions for me. Or I would just wait to decide on life-changing choices until someone told me, "If you wait long enough to make a decision, time will make it for you. You will not have a choice." When I acknowledged the truth of this statement, I decided that life was too short not to make my own decisions. Oh, I still lack confidence in myself, but once I have sought wise counsel and doubled checked with God, I move forward. Actually, it's been much easier than living a life of indecision.

Share how you typically make decisions in your life:

_____

_____

In today's closing section, I want to confirm that God doesn't mind when we are uncertain or second-guess ourselves. He doesn't frown and say, "Hey, I told you. Now I don't want to hear another peep out of you!"

Read the following Scriptures about John the Baptist: John 1:29-34.

What did John the Baptist declare about Jesus?

_____

Read Matthew 11:2-6, 11. Where was John the Baptist in these verses?

_____

Why did John send his disciples to ask Jesus?

_____

What response did Jesus give?

_____

In verse 11, how did Jesus commend John the Baptist?

_____

Jesus did not express disapproval of John for his questions. Jesus reconfirmed He was the Son of God by the miracles that were performed. Christ understood that John the Baptist sat in a dark, dank prison cell with probable death looming before him. Jesus instructed John's disciples to report to John the Baptist all the miracles they had witnessed. This reconfirmed He was indeed the promised Messiah. Then Christ praised John with the words, "I tell you the truth: Among those born of women there has not risen anyone greater than John the Baptist." Not bad for a guy who second-guessed the deity of Christ Jesus.

Let's spend prayer time with Jesus—who is with us.

Lord Jesus,

Faith Fun
Tonight put a dry towel outside on the lawn. Check in the morning to feel if it is wet or dry. Repeat the experiment tomorrow night. Would you use this method to check on God's will or would you request a different type of "fleece"?

Your mighty warrior, _____
                        Sign your name

Faith Finale!
The Lord is with you, mighty warrior.   Judges 6:12

Day 4 – **What If?**

Lord God,

I admit that I am afraid to trust You. I worry that You will test my faith by allowing hard circumstances in my life. Help me to grow in faith beyond this senseless apprehension.

In Jesus' name, Amen

"Are you afraid of snakes?" my friend's son asked with a smirk. I felt a surge of fear at the question. Then I noticed his hands hidden below the kitchen counter. I swallowed hard as I realized he probably held a snake in his twelve-year-old hands. What if I answered, "Yes"? *What if,* he tossed it in my lap to watch my horrified reaction?

"Not much," I answered.

Sure enough, he came around the corner holding a wiggly, white and orange snake. However, my answer had clearly deflated his mischievous intentions. He brought the harmless critter closer, but held it tightly in his hands. Bored with the result, he left the room with the snake in tow to find another surprised soul with a phobia of snakes. I breathed a sigh of relief and unclenched my sweaty palms.

Don't we often react in the same manner with God? We fear that if we decide to trust Him, He will allow something horrible in our lives. We ask ourselves all sorts of fear-filled questions. *What if God sends me to Africa to be a missionary? What if I get cancer? What if He wants me to live a life of poverty like Mother Teresa? What if He takes one of my children? What if He desires I stay single? What if? What if? What if?*

Do you relate? List any "what if" fears that haunt your thoughts when you ponder trusting God.

_____

_____

My friend, let's take a stroll through a few Scriptures and see what we can discover about faith and our "what ifs."

Read Daniel 3:13-18.
What did Nebuchadnezzar threaten Shadrach, Meshach, and Abednego with if they refused to worship his gods?

_____

Who did Shadrach, Meshach and Abednego decide to trust regardless of the "what if" that faced them?

_____

How did they respond to Nebuchadnezzar's threat in verses 17, 18?

_____

Shadrach, Meshach, and Abednego faced an enormous uncertainty. They had no promise from their unseen God. Yet, they chose to hold onto their faith. They defied Nebuchadnezzar and refused to acquiesce to his demands. Not one of the three men held a guarantee that God would rescue them. However, each of them decided that God was worthy of his faith and trust—whether they lived or died. How do you think you would have responded to Nebuchadnezzar? Explain your answer.

_____

_____

Now, let's see the result of Shadrach, Meshach, and Abednego's trust. Read Daniel 3:19-28. What occurred when Shadrach, Meshach, and Abednego were thrown into the furnace?

_____

What did Nebuchadnezzar see when he looked into the fire?

_____

Whom did Nebuchadnezzar declare the three men served?

_____

Rewrite verse 28 in your own words:

_____

_____

Nebuchadnezzar experienced quite a shock as he watched the three men walking around in the fire. He realized that Shadrach, Meshach, and Abednego had faced their "what ifs" about God, but still chose to trust and serve Him—regardless of the result.

How do you think we influence others when we choose to trust God despite our fears?

_____

_____

Faith Fiction
If we trust God, our greatest fear will come to fruition.

51

When I watch other people face their fears and move in faith with God, it inspires me. I enjoy reading biographies of faithful Christians such as Oswald Chambers, Joni Eareckson Tada, and Corrie Ten Boom who have faced their doubts and fears. Their stories of devotion encourage me to let go of my anxiety of the future and to trust God.

Let's move to the New Testament. We're going to see how the disciple Thomas faced his own fear with a shrug of resolution and the decision to follow Jesus even to death.

Read John 11:11-16. What did Thomas say to the rest of the disciples?

_____

Perhaps you recall studying John 11 in Week 1, Day 5. Quickly scan through it again. Instead of his own death, what did Thomas witness?

_____

Thomas witnessed Lazarus being raised from the dead. Can you imagine if Thomas had determined the danger was too great? His "what if" could have prevented him from going with Jesus and missing one of the greatest opportunities to have his faith increased.

Can you share a time when you might have missed an opportunity to increase your faith because of your fear of a "what if?"

_____

_____

Faith Fact
Faith recognizes the "what ifs" and still trusts God.

If yes, do you now regret your lack of trust? Why or why not?

_____

_____

When you experience a "what if," take encouragement from Thomas's resolution to follow Jesus in spite of the fear of the unknown. He didn't stay in his misgiving, but allowed Christ to take him to a new level of belief. Let's not settle into our qualms, but move on to decision and belief.

Thomas struggled with a pessimistic outlook. I want to examine another situation in which he allowed doubt to envelop him. The rumor of Christ's resurrection surrounded Thomas, but he refused to believe. Read John 20:24-28.

What did Thomas doubt?

_____

What did Thomas say he would need before he believed the other disciples?

_____

How did Jesus counter Thomas's doubt one week later?

_____

Write Thomas's response. (verse 28)

_____

_____

Thomas doubted the resurrection of Jesus Christ. He didn't believe his friends, but retorted, "Unless I see the nail marks in his hands and put my finger where the nails were, and put my hand into his side, I will not believe it" (verse 25). One week later, it was a different story. Then he declared to Jesus, "My Lord and my God!" (verse 25).

Do you have difficulty believing Jesus Christ arose from the dead?

_____

If yes, I have a "what if" for you to consider. Knowing that Thomas doubted, what if you discovered that once Thomas believed it, there were no more "what ifs" for him.

Historians report that after this incident in John 20, Thomas preached the deity of Jesus Christ throughout Persia. He based his confidence on the certainty of the sacrificial death and resurrection of Jesus to which he had been an eyewitness. In addition, Thomas is credited with the founding of Christianity in India. He no longer doubted or held "what ifs." Thomas is believed to have been pierced with a sword—a martyr for his faith.[2]

Why would Thomas die for his faith?

_____

How does the example of Thomas affect your own doubts and "what ifs"? Write a prayer to Jesus concerning your fear of the "what ifs" in life.

_____

_____

Faith Fun

Write an acronym for the words *fear* and *faith*. For example:

Faith F
Erases E
Anxious A
Reflections R

_____ F
_____ E
_____ A
_____ R

_____ F
_____ A
_____ I
_____ T
_____ H

Faith Finale!

Stop doubting and believe (John 20:27).

Jesus, my Lord and my God,

In Your name, Amen

Day 5 – **Sprouts Under the Sink**

Lord Jesus,

When the darkness of doubt hinders my faith, shine Your light into my life. Help the seeds of my faith to sprout. Keep growing my faith with each step I take in my journey with You.

In Your name, Amen.

Years ago, I grew food under my sink. Behind the closed cabinet doors, in the dark, grew a wholesome source of nutrition—sprouts. I placed seeds in a jar and filled it with water. I would set it under the kitchen sink with a thin cloth placed over the top of the jar, secured by a rubber band. After the first day, I would then rinse and drain the sprouts twice a day. Within three to four days, the seeds metamorphosed into sprouts. Then, I needed to place them in sunlight for just a few hours. The light increased the development of additional vitamins. Bingo! The tiny seeds had developed into delicious bean sprouts ready to garnish soups or sandwiches.

Sometimes that's how our faith grows too. It sits silently, unknown to us. But slowly, the Living Water soaks into our heart. Time passes. Then we gaze into the mirror of our souls and realize our faith has sprouted and we are ready to face the world. Today, we will see an example of this happening in the life of Nicodemus. Let's see how Nicodemus' faith progressed and use it as an example to encourage us.

Read John 2:23—3:17. Describe Nicodemus (verses 1, 10):

_____

At what time of the day did Nicodemus come to speak with Jesus?

_____

Why do you think Nicodemus came in the darkness of the night?

_____

What did Nicodemus confess to know about Jesus? Why? (verse 2)

_____

_____

Nicodemus was a Pharisee. The Pharisees were a very large and influential group who held sway in the religious and political arenas during New Testament times. People respected them for their knowledge and devout religious behaviors. Nicodemus had a tiny seed of faith. He believed God was with Jesus because of the miracles that had occurred in Jerusalem. However, because Nicodemus did not want others to see him speak with Jesus, he came to Him in the darkness of night.

Can you describe a time when you were scared to show your faith in front of others?

_____

_____

Faith Fiction
It's easy to display our faith when others are watching us.

Christ taught Nicodemus a few basic elements about the kingdom of God. Perplexed, Nicodemus questioned Him, "How can a man be born when he is old? . . . How can this be?" (verses 4, 9).

Jesus didn't go into great theological detail to answer the questions. He didn't break open the Torah and Jewish commentaries. Jesus explained the kingdom of God to Nicodemus with the simple bottom line: "For God so loved the world that he gave his one and only Son, that whoever believes in him shall not perish but have eternal life" (John 3:16).

The following verses in this passage do not relay that Nicodemus accepted Jesus' words as truth. All we know is that he took the conversation back out into the night to ponder. His seed of faith had been watered and now needed time to sprout.

We're going to leave Nicodemus for a while, but we'll come back to him. However, let's discover a few things about darkness, water, light, and faith.

Read the following verses and underline what Jesus states about Himself.

I am the living bread that came down from heaven. If anyone eats of this bread, he will live forever. John 6:51

When Jesus spoke again to the people, he said, "I am the light of the world. Whoever follows me will never walk in darkness, but will have the light of life." John 8:12

Jesus answered her, "If you knew the gift of God and who it is that asks you for a drink, you would have asked him and he would have given you living water." John 4:10

I have come into the world as a light, so that no one who believes in me should stay in darkness. John 12:46

What elements do these verses contain that are part of the process of turning seeds into sprouts?

_____

_____

Our faith goes through a process similar to the bean sprouts under the sink. Faith always begins in darkness. But Jesus, who is the Living Water, permeates Himself into us as we grow in Him. Our faith comes out of the darkness and into the light. As our faith sprouts and becomes more evident, we will be able to share the Living Bread with others.

Faith Fact
Our faith grows and bears fruit as we get to know Jesus more intimately.

To help increase our knowledge of Jesus, note what else Jesus declared about Himself. Write down how each of these applies to your own life.

John 10:9 _____

John 10:11 _____

John 11:25 _____

John 14:6 _____

John 15:5 _____

Let's return to Nicodemus and see what happened after he walked into the darkness of night after speaking with Jesus. Read John 7:41-52.

Who was Nicodemus with in these verses? (See verses 45, 47)

_____

In verse 50, what two descriptions are given about Nicodemus?

_____

How would you describe the response of Nicodemus?

_____

As we see him boldly challenging his colleagues, the Pharisees, what appears to have happened since he went to Jesus under the cover of darkness?

_____

Read Jeremiah 29:13 and then apply it to Nicodemus.

_____

_____

I don't know how that verse affects you, but it makes my heart leap. My heart rejoices that even if I seek the Lord, I will find Him. Describe your own thoughts on Jeremiah 29:13.

_____

_____

Faith Fun
Just for fun, try producing some sprouts. Place five kidney or pinto beans in a small jar. Cover them with water and place a cloth or paper towel over the opening. Keep them in a dark place. The next day drain, rinse, and drain the sprouts. Continue to rinse and drain the sprouts for three to four days. Watch and see what happens.

As we close this week's study, we find Nicodemus once again displaying his faith more boldly than ever. Read John 19:38-42. What did Nicodemus accomplish with Joseph of Arimathea?

_____

Nicodemus and Joseph of Arimathea, although afraid, chose to ask for the body of Jesus. They lavishly prepared His body with expensive spices and laid Him in a tomb. Their tiny faith spoke volumes about their real hearts and it lives on more than two thousands years later. A seed of faith sprouted out of the darkness into an everlasting testimony. *The Life Application Bible* states,

> Joseph of Arimathea and Nicodemus were secret followers of Jesus. They were afraid to make this allegiance known because of their positions in the Jewish community. Joseph was a leader and honored member of the Jewish council. Nicodemus, also a member of the council, had come to Jesus by night (John 3:1) and later tried to defend him before the other religious leaders (John 7:50-52). Yet they risked their reputations to provide for Jesus' burial. Are you a secret believer? Do you hide your faith from your friends and fellow workers? This is an appropriate time to step out of hiding and let others know whom you follow.[3]

Close this week with a prayer to Jesus the risen Christ. Let your faith sprout to new acts of greatness!

Faith Finale!

"You will seek me and find me when you seek me with all your heart. I will be found by you," declares the LORD. Jeremiah 29:13a

Faith Seed Thoughts & Prayers – **Review Week 2**
Journal your thoughts about how this week's lesson applied to you personally.

1 Ortberg, John. *If You Want To Walk On Water, You've Got To Get Out Of The Boat,* (Grand Rapids, MI, Zondervan
   Publishing House, 2001), 25-26.

2 Zacharias, Ravi. *Walking From East to West*, (Grand Rapids, MI: Zondervan Corp., 2006.)

3 *Life Application Bible* (Wheaton, IL: Tyndale House, 1991). 1925.

Week 3
Amazing Faith

Day 1 – **Who Is Like Our God?**

Lord God,

Open my eyes and my heart to understand that You are an awesome God. Increase my knowledge of Your mighty strength and goodness. As my knowledge increases, I pray that it will enable me to trust You more.

In Jesus' name, Amen

I lived in Okinawa, Japan for almost three years. Japan handed me a religious culture shock. The Japanese society follows a variety of religious beliefs, but their two primary belief systems are Shintoism and Buddhism. Both are separate religions, yet they have become intertwined in the Japanese society. In brief, the concept consists of multitudes of spirits who can bring both good and evil to a person or nation. Any natural object is inhabited by a spirit or god.

In each restaurant I visited, the gods were displayed prominently on a counter. Most Japanese homes included a special shelf for the "family" gods. Along the roadsides, small shrines to various gods and ancestral spirits accumulated food and flowers people brought as offerings to their god.

As I drove through the narrow streets, I saw people bowed down on their knees in adoration to a stone statue. I found it difficult to fathom why someone would worship an inanimate object.

However, idol worship is not new. Almost since the beginning of time, people have worshiped worthless idols. Let's investigate biblical history to help us grasp the prevalence of gods versus our God. As we study the differences, our faith in the one true Lord God will increase.

Read Genesis 28:20-22. Write down the gist of what Jacob vowed to God.

_____

Read Genesis 31:11-19. Who was speaking to Jacob in verse 13?

_____

How did Rachel and Leah respond? Specifically, note what they stated about God.

_____

What did Rachel do in verse 19?

_____

God spoke loud and clear to Jacob, "Now leave this land at once and go back to your native land" (verse 13b). Jacob's wives, Rachel and Leah, agreed to move without any hesitation. However, for some reason, Rachel stole her father's household gods.

These household gods were associated with the ability to provide luck and prosperity. They were also thought to give divine guidance—sort of a fortune-telling prophecy. *The Life Application Bible Notes* offers this explanation: "Many people kept small wooden or metal idols ("gods") in their homes. These idols were called *teraphim,* and they were thought to protect the home and offer advice in times of need."[1]

Although she acknowledged the true God, Rachel's faith must have wavered regarding the gods of her childhood. Did she think, "Just in case, I'll pack these, too, for they might bring us good luck, and Daddy Laban can't use them to find us"? So, she tucked them out of sight from Jacob and rode off into the sunset.

But Laban still tracked down the runaway family. (Obviously, he didn't need household gods to track the family across the hill country.) Now let's continue reading Genesis 31:25-35.

In verse 29, who did Laban acknowledge spoke a warning to him?

_____

What question did Laban ask Jacob in verse 30?

_____

How did Rachel hide the gods?

_____

What lie did she tell her father?

_____

The true God warned Laban not to say anything to Jacob, either good or bad. What a predicament Laban was in when he finally caught up with Jacob's caravan. It makes me smile when I think of him wanting to lambaste Jacob. Instead, I imagine he wrung his hands nervously as he asked wimpishly, "Now you have gone off because you longed to return to your father's house. But why did you steal my gods?"

We might think Rachel risked a lot for a bunch of wooden or metal trinkets that held no true worth for their household move or their spiritual journey. Yet, in our modern culture, there are things people hold onto with a superstitious belief for good luck or for guidance, aren't there? Maybe it's a family heirloom, a special pair of sports socks, or a daily horoscope. Let's take a moment and list a few things that might come to mind.

1. _____

2. _____

3. _____

4. _____

It's probable that without even being aware, we say or do things that reveal a certain lack of trust in the Lord. Many of my friends check their horoscope without a thought of how that shows a lack of faith in the sovereignty of God.

Recently, I realized that my good- intentioned remark of, "Good luck!" actually displayed this same lack of faith. I have been trying to substitute my traditional habit of saying, "Good luck" with "Be blessed." I know this seems like such a minor thing in my walk of faith, yet somehow, I personally need to be more conscious of my own "household gods."

Before we close today's lesson, look to see what the Bible has to say about any type of false gods or idols. Read Exodus 20:3-4 and paraphrase the second commandment.

Faith Fact
There is only one true Living God.

Read Jeremiah 10:3-5. These verses are God's words quoted by the prophet Jeremiah.

Below mark an X on the line by the word describing what might have been God's tone of voice.

_____

Sorrow   Kindness   Pleading   Sarcasm   Chiding   Encouragement

Now write out Jeremiah 10:6.

_____

_____

Jeremiah closes this proclamation from God with his own words, "No one is like you, O LORD, you are great, and your name is mighty in power." No wooden and straw scarecrows for old Jeremiah, or for us. We will believe in only the Lord God.

In your opinion, why do people put their faith in inanimate objects of nature?

_____

_____

Thankfully, we know the true Living God. Let's commit to complete dependence on His faithfulness in our lives. Let's cast aside anything in our lives that could be construed as a "household god," whether it's a family heirloom, a bank account, a horoscope, or just a trinket which causes us to be superstitious. Let's rely on God alone.

63

As we close today's lesson, let's read Isaiah 46:9 in the margin. I believe it is a fitting response to the nonsense that "all religions lead to god."

It makes me want to shout, "Amen and Amen!" Doesn't it you? Let's take a few minutes to ponder the truth of this lesson. Write a prayer asking the Lord to help you have stronger faith in His ability to care and guide you on this journey called life.

Lord God,

I am God, and there is no other; I am God, and there is none like me.
Isaiah 46:9

In Jesus name, Amen

Faith Fun
Read Acts 17:16, 22-27. Think about your hometown. If there were an "Unknown God", what would it be? How does worship of that unknown god affect the community? The families? Worship of the true God?

Faith Finale!
No one is like you, O Lord; you are great, and your name is mighty in power.
Jeremiah 10:6

Day 2 – **A Walk Through Nature**

Lord God,

Open my eyes to Your wonders. Forgive me for taking so many things for granted each day that in reality are amazing creations formed by Your hands. As I watch for nature to display Your wonder, increase my faith in You, my Creator.

In Jesus' name, Amen

Modern technology is amazing. I remember as a child watching high-speed photography of a flower that budded and bloomed. The photography captured days of nature's movement and beauty, so that in a few minutes I could see and understand what took place in my garden.

Even though we can see pictures, movies, and read books on the wonder of nature, there is nothing like experiencing it for ourselves. Today, we are going to allow God's handiwork in nature to amaze and strengthen our faith. Let's allow our mind's eye and our imagination to kick into high gear. Let's open our eyes to a universe that declares the glory of a Creator—our Lord Jesus Christ.

First, let's reflect on how often we actually take a good look at nature. On the list below, note how long it's been since you . . .

Walked in a park _____

Went to a zoo _____

Hiked a mountain path _____

Picnicked on a blanket _____

Swam in a lake or ocean _____

Saw a shooting star _____

Gazed at the night sky _____

Heard a rushing river _____

Gardened _____

Played in the rain _____

So often, we miss the glory of God in nature. Stress and busyness hinder our senses from recognizing the beauty of God's creation. We allow life's mundane tasks to strip us of opportunities to increase our faith. The earth's Creator gifted us with the five senses—sight, hearing, touch, smell, and touch. He did this so we could experience His character and personality.

Let's see what Scripture says to us about building our faith in God by observing nature.

First, let's look at the Creator of nature. Read Genesis 1:1-25. Fill in the blanks of the following verses.

Verse 1: In the beginning _____ _____ the _____ and the _____.

Verse 25b: And _____ _____that it was _____.

Read John 1:1-3, 14 from the *Amplified Bible* below.

> *IN THE beginning [before all time] was the Word (Christ), and the Word was with God, and the Word was God Himself. ² He was present originally with God. ³ All things were made and came into existence through Him; and without Him was not even one thing made that has come into being.*
>
> *And the Word (Christ) became flesh (human, incarnate) and tabernacled (fixed His tent of flesh, lived awhile) among us; and we [actually] saw His glory (His honor, His majesty), such glory as an only begotten son receives from his father, full of grace (favor, loving-kindness) and truth.*

Jesus Christ is not only our Savior, but He is also our Creator. In the beginning, He created the beauty of the world, so our eyes would be open to His reality. Theologians call this aspect of faith *general revelation.* General revelation provides us a universal aspect of God. We have the ability to glimpse God's knowledge, creativity, and provision through the observation of the physical universe.

Let's take a walk through God's nature park—the universe and our planet. Read aloud Psalm 104:1-31.

Jot down God's activities as Caretaker that are poetically illustrated in Psalm 104.

_____

_____

Our God rules nature; nature does not control God. The Creator spread out the stars in the heavens and set the foundations of the earth. He covered it with water and then set the boundaries of the seas. He assigned the rivers to their places in the mountains. He provides water to all living things. God causes grass and plants to grow. He provides nutrition and lodging for His creatures. He enables us to cultivate and work the earth, so we, in return, will glorify Him.

Share your thoughts on Psalm 104. Does the glory of God's handiwork increase your faith in God's ability to care for you? If yes, why?

_____

_____

How many are your works, O LORD! In wisdom you made them all; the earth is full of your creatures . . . May the glory of the LORD endure forever; may the LORD rejoice in his works."
Psalm 104:24, 31

My faith increases when I stop to think about the miraculous beauty of nature. If God can take care of the mighty heavens and the spinning earth, then I *know* He is able to take care of me. The Lord has given us proof through nature that He exists and that he provides for His creation. He particularly cares for us!

Read and ponder Psalm 8:3, 4 in the margin. Describe the truth and hope found in these verses.

_____

_____

When I consider your heavens, the work of your fingers, the moon and the stars, which you have set in place, what is man that you are mindful of him, the son of man that you care for him?
Psalm 8:3, 4

Now read Psalm 19:1-4 and give a brief summary of each verse.

Verse 1: _____

Verse 2: _____

Verse 3: _____

Verse 4: _____

Read Romans 1:20. What does verse 20 clearly state?

_____

Faith Fact
The beauty of nature points us toward God's glory.

My friend, let's open our eyes to the evidence that God provides. We are without excuse, if we choose to place our faith in anything other than the loving God who cares for us. Let's take a moment to thank our amazing Creator, Provider, and

Savior—Jesus Christ—using a paraphrased Psalm 8:3, 4 as a springboard for our worship.

Lord Jesus,

When I consider Your heavens, the work of Your fingers, the moon and the stars, which You have set in place, what am I that You are mindful of me, and that You care for me?

In Your glorious name, Amen

Faith Finale!
The heavens declare the glory of God; the skies proclaim the work of his hands. Day after day they pour forth speech; night after night they display knowledge. There is no speech or language where their voice is not heard. Psalm 19:1-3

Day 3 – **The Womb of Wonder**

Lord Jesus,

Forgive me for not accepting how You formed me. As I study Your design for others and myself, help me to understand that You created me exactly as You desired. Help me, by faith, to trust Your hand in every aspect of my physical body and the physical bodies of those that I love.

In Your name, I pray, Amen

Faith Fun
Take a faith field trip. Set aside some time this week to enjoy God's creation. Take a notebook and write about the amazing things that you see, hear, feel, touch, and taste.

Faith Fiction
Modern science explains nature's entire phenomenon.

Last night I sat mesmerized by a National Geographic television show, *In the Womb*. The 90-minute episode provided an inside view of a baby forming in its mother's womb. Specialized cameras and ultrasound equipment explored the womb and the outside world from the baby's point of view. Fascinating! However, every few minutes the commentator would admit that there were certain things they could not explain. For example, why does the baby open its eyes in the pitch-black womb? Or what signals the mother's body to go into labor with birthing contractions? Even with specialized 3-D and 4-D equipment, science cannot explain all the miracles of life.

Only God knows and understands all the answers. We all have questions. Why are my thighs heavy and my sister's thin? Why did I inherit the big nose from grandpa's side of the family, instead of delicate grandma's? Why did I develop cancer? Why was my child born with a cleft palate? God is silent on His genetic choices for our bodies. God doesn't give us the reasons for how He created us or for the twists and turns our physical bodies take as we age.

What would be your top three questions you would like to ask God about your physical body?

1. _____

2. _____

3. _____

Today we are going to study a fellow named Job. (Job is pronounced with a long ō, by the way.) The name "Job" translates from the Hebrew as "the hated or persecuted one." Allow me to give you a bit of history on Job. The book of Job is thought to be one of the first books written in the Bible. The author is unknown; however, it is commonly considered that Moses recorded this biography.

The story begins with Job's everyday life: family, faith, work, and just the ordinary, mundane happenings in life. (This is recorded in Job 1:1-5.) The following verses and the next chapter describe Job's life falling apart: his wealth disappears, his children are killed, and he comes down with a chronic debilitating illness.

Read Job 2:7-19. Describe Job's physical condition.

_____

Read Job 23:1-5. Describe how you think Job feels as he spouts these words.

_____

Have you ever felt this way? If yes, when and why?

_____

Approximately thirty-nine chapters allow us to see Job's hurt, his confusion, and his questions. Then God's voice rumbles down to Job. Scan through chapters 38-42. What type of questions does God ask Job?

_____

Read Job 42:1-6. What is Job's response to God's questioning?

_____

What would you have said to God?

_____

_____

I think I might have replied with words similar to Exodus 15:11. Read these words in the margin.

I have always been horrified that I might age as my grandmothers did. When I was a little girl, I would stare at my paternal grandmother's heavy legs mapped with varicose veins. I would rub my own lithe legs and think, *Yuck, my legs will never look like that!* My eyes have always been my best feature, but my maternal grandmother's eyes carried large bluish-black circles underneath them. I was certain my beautiful eyes could never develop those horrid bags. Guess what? I developed both as middle age overtook my youth. Horrors!

Then I think about a few children that I know. One born with autism. Another baby born without hands due to amniotic band syndrome. Another friend's child has several severe physical handicaps. When I consider these little ones, my own physical disappointments are meaningless. Yet, what would God have us all know about His wonderful works in creating every single person? Read Ecclesiastes 11:5. How does this Scripture resemble the response of our Lord to Job?

_____

Even though we cannot understand why these things happen anymore than Job could comprehend life's struggles, Scripture assures us none of this is a surprise to our God.

Take a moment to study a few New Testament Scriptures. Read below the Scripture passages and then match the verse reference to the correct passage.

Revelation 21:4
John 9:2, 3
Romans 8:28

His disciples asked him, "Rabbi, who sinned, this man, or his parents, that he was born blind?" "Neither this man nor his parents sinned," said Jesus, "but this happened so that the work of God might be displayed in his life."

And we know that in all things God works for the good of those who love him, who have been called according to his purpose.

He will wipe every tear from their eyes. There will be no more death or mourning or crying or pain, for the old order of things has passed away.

Explain how the above verses will strengthen your faith:

_____

_____

God's will for our lives is always tied to His goodness, His sovereignty, and His love for us. We might not understand why He created us the way He did, but there is comfort in knowing He planned it. Read the following verses in the margin. Then fill in your name in the blanks of the same paraphrased verses.

For God created _____ inmost being; He knit _____ together in my mother's womb.
Before God formed _____ in the womb He knew _____, before _____ was born God set her apart.

For you created my inmost being; you knit me together in my mother's womb.
Psalm 139:13

Before I formed you in the womb I knew you, before you were born I set you apart.
Jeremiah 1:5a

71

Faith Fun
Rent *National Geographic's* "In the Womb" DVD at your local video store. Memorize Psalm139:13 and Jeremiah 1:5. As you watch, consider these two verses and praise the Lord who formed you.

Lord God, my Creator,

I thank You, in Jesus' name, Amen.

Faith Finale!
From birth I have relied on you; you brought me forth from my mother's womb. I will ever praise you. Psalm 71:6

Faith Fact
God knows the true and intricate details of our bodies.

Day 4 – **Vanished Amazement**

Dear Lord,

Even when I see the glory of Your hands in nature, my faith struggles at times. Although I understand the wonder of the womb, I still ask, "Why?" Forgive my lack of faith in You. Strengthen my faith, so You may work more powerfully in my life.

In Jesus' name, Amen.

Bubbles amaze my grandchildren. To the children's great entertainment, the bubbles float through the air. The kids scamper around, attempting to pop the prism of colors before they drop to the floor. Children find wonder and amazement in simple things.

However, as children mature into adulthood, it is harder to excite them. It takes the spectacular to wow people. I find this true in my own life. Most things that intrigued me as a child have long since been discarded. The thrill of riding a tricycle disappeared as I pedaled my bicycle on the pavement. The bicycle grew rusty when I obtained my driver's license. And so it goes.

Faith can follow the same pathway. List three experiences that would increase your faith at this point in your spiritual journey.

1. _____

2. _____

3. _____

Read the following Bible passages and note what caused the people's amazement.

Mark 5:1-20 _____

Luke 5:18-26 _____

Luke 6:17-19 _____

Luke 7:11-17 _____

These passages describe for us the miracles Jesus performed. The people were wowed. They stood astonished. They sang His praises. Amazement filled them, but only for a short while. Sadly, the miraculous events turned into popped bubbles of ho-hum belief. Let's see what happens to faith when we depend on the signs and wonders from God.

Match the following references with the correct passage of Scripture.

Psalm 78:11   Psalm 78:32
John 7:4, 5   John 12:37

Even after Jesus had done all these miraculous signs in their presence, they still would not believe in him.

They forgot what he had done, the wonders he had shown them.

No one who wants to become a public figure acts in secret. Since you are doing these things, show yourself to the world. For even his own brothers did not believe in him.

In spite of all this, they kept on sinning; in spite of his wonders, they did not believe.

Faith Fiction
An amazing miracle will keep my faith strong.

It seems the familiar phrase, "familiarity breeds contempt," rings true in our journey of faith too. For myself, I tend to forget how His grace and mercy have changed my life. He took me from spiritual darkness to walk in the truth of His light. Yet, the reality of this miracle fades and I want Jesus to show Himself mighty again and again.

Read Mark 6:5, 6. Fill in the blanks.
"He could not do any _____ there, except lay his hands on a few sick people and heal them. And _____ was _____ at their _____ _____ _____."

Do you think Jesus has been restricted by your lack of faith? If yes, explain.

_____

Read John 6:60-68. What question did Jesus ask His disciples? Why?

_____

Have you ever considered giving up on your spiritual journey because it seemed too hard?

_____

_____

Our faith must be based on Jesus and His Words of truth—whether we like them or not. We cannot allow our desire for signs and wonders to override our slow step-by-step growth of faith. Let's speak with our Lord Jesus today about the tendency of our faith to disappear. Let's commit to Him to build our faith on His words of truth—one verse at a time.

Lord Jesus,

I ask this in Your holy name, Amen

Faith Finale!

Simon Peter answered him, "Lord, to whom shall we go? You have the words of eternal life. We believe and know that you are the Holy One of God." John 6:68, 69

Day 5 – **Let's Amaze Him!**

Lord Jesus,

I desire for my faith to grow strong. I want to amaze you with my faith. Grant me Your Holy Spirit to teach me Your Words and to strengthen my faith. Lord, grow my faith to amazing heights.

In Your name, Amen

My husband installed an automatic closure on my oldest son's bedroom door. When my son left the door open—it closed. We couldn't stand the stress of his messy bedroom. Clothes, sports equipment, and school papers littered the floor. We argued, begged, and punished—all to no avail. His room remained a pigsty. We finally decided the stress wasn't worth it. We conceded, waved the white flag, and purchased the necessary hardware to hide the eyesore. The automatic closure ended the war of wills. We saved our strength for the larger battles of parenting teens. However, this was not the end of the story.

"Your son is *so* helpful when he stays at our house. He helps me clean-up all the other guy's messes," said a neighbor. "I wish I could teach my son to pick-up after himself."

"Oh! That's wonderful," I responded. However, inside I thought, "*Whose* kid are you talking about?"

My child amazed her. I was proud that my neighbor knew he was a great kid. My tunnel vision had allowed me to see only his messy room, but now I saw through the eyes of another adult. My son amazed me too.

Today our faith lesson is learning we, too, can amaze our Father. Are you ready?

Faith Fun
Purchase a bottle of children's bubbles. Enjoy blowing bubbles and watch how quickly they pop. Keep them on hand to remind yourself how quickly our memory fades concerning God's works in our lives.

Faith Fiction
Jesus was never amazed by anything.

Read Luke 7:1-10. Who asked Jesus to come heal his servant?

_____

Whom did he send to ask Jesus?

_____

Paraphrase the Roman centurion's statements in verses 6-8.
What was Jesus' initial reaction? What did He say to the crowd following him?

_____

_____

Finally, what was the result of the centurion's faith?

_____

The Roman centurion, a Gentile, asked the Jewish elder to go on his behalf to ask Jesus to come heal his ailing servant. However, after he thought it over, the man realized Jesus did not even need to come to his house to heal. He hurriedly sent friends to Jesus essentially to say, "Hey, just command it and it will happen!" Amazing—that's what Jesus thought: "I tell you, I have not found such great faith even in Israel" (verse 9b).

Explain how you feel about the possibility of being able to amaze Jesus with your faith.

_____

_____

Place a check beside the things you believe you might need to do to amaze Him.

_____ Heal the sick
_____ Trust Him in a crisis
_____ Raise the dead
_____ Respect your husband
_____ Witness to a co-worker
_____ Believe He loves You
_____ Trust your children to Him
_____ Walk on water

I believe, as I had tunnel vision with my son's messiness, likewise, we have tunnel vision when it comes to our own faith. At least, I do. I think I need to do something spectacular—something mighty and wonderful for the whole world to see and then God will be aware of my faith. But, that's not the case. Private acts of faith stir the heart of God much more than great spectacles of faith. Still don't believe it? Let's reach out for a little more assurance for our little mustard seed amazement.

Read Matthew 9:18-22. Fill in the blanks of the following verses. Just then a woman who had been subject to bleeding for twelve years _____ _____ _____ him and _____ the edge of his cloak. She said to herself, "_____ _____ ___ touch his cloak, I will be healed." (Matthew 9:20, 21).

This unnamed woman didn't display any confidence in her faith. She tiptoed behind Jesus. She didn't clutch His cloak in desperation, but she gingerly reached out to touch it. She thought, "*If only I* can touch his cloak, I will be healed."

What did Jesus say, and then what happened? (verse 22)

_____

Will you believe "if only I" and then fill in the blanks with your name?

Jesus turned and saw _____. "Take heart, _____," he
said,   Your Name   Your Name
"_____ your faith has _____."
      Your Name   Fill in your area of need

As I ponder the centurion and the sick woman, it seems that what pleases God is our attempt to believe in His character and ability. God has never asked me to raise the dead or walk on water. But He has asked that I reach out and touch the cloak of His strength, compassion, and love. I think I can do that. Can you?

Share your thoughts on touching His invisible cloak.

_____

Faith Fact
Private and public acts of faith please God.

77

Read Matthew 25:21. How would you apply this verse to the subject of faith?

_____

If we attempt to stretch our faith to please God, He will say with a smile, "Well done, my good and faithful servant." Then He will ask us to believe more, trust more, and reach out in faith repeatedly.

And best of all we'll hear Jesus say, "Let's celebrate together!" That will be amazing!

Friend, close this week with a prayer to reach out in faith to a God who loves to be amazed by our acts of faith.

Lord Jesus,

In Your compassionate name, Amen

Faith Finale!
When Jesus heard this, he was amazed. Turning to the crowd, he said, "I tell you, I haven't seen faith like this in all of Israel!" Luke 7:9, NLT

Faith Seed Thoughts & Prayers – **Review Week 3**

Journal your thoughts about how this week's lessons applied to you personally.

Faith Fun
Let's amaze!
- Compliment three people who do things that amaze you.
- Do something out of your ordinary routine to amaze someone you love.
- Reach out and touch the invisible cloak of Jesus in three small areas of faith.

1 *Life Application Bible*, c1991 by Tyndale House Publishers, Inc., Wheaton, IL 60189. Notes and Bible helps 1991 by Tyndale House Publishers, Inc. Database c NavPress Software.

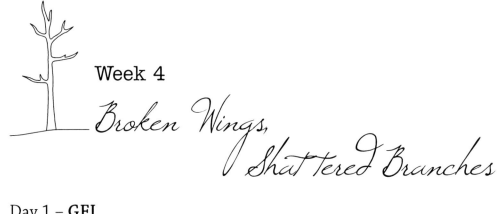

Week 4
Broken Wings, Shattered Branches

Day 1 – **GFI**

Lord God,

I prefer those times when my life goes smoothly. However, I ask for an extra measure of faith when my life takes a twist and moves off the planned path. Teach me to trust Your sovereignty in my life.

In Jesus' name, Amen

I pulled in the driveway grateful to be home after a five-day conference. I pressed the remote and the garage door rolled open. Blood trickled toward me as I stepped from my car. I immediately knew what had happened—the freezer had gone out. All the meat had thawed and the bloody, watery juices had drained out of the freezer into a maroon stream that slowly ran toward the driveway.

Mark, my husband, was out of town. I stood in my garage disgusted and slightly freaked out. What did I do? Of course, I called my husband for help. I didn't care if it was late and there was a three-hour time difference.
He patiently said, "Check the GFI."

"The what?"

"The ground fault interrupter. It's in the outlet where the freezer is plugged in."

Sure enough, the GFI had tripped and shut down the freezer. Nothing was wrong with the freezer, except now it had hundreds of dollars of rotting meat sitting inside it.

Because of a GFI, my evening turned from one of anticipated relaxation to hours of vexing cleanup.

Isn't our faith like that, too? We are believing and trusting the Lord, when all of sudden something happens—GFI—God Faith Interrupter. Our faith trips and we melt down like a gallon of vanilla ice cream in a hot garage.

Thankfully, God provided many examples of heroes of faith that had God Faith Interrupters too. But then, stumbled into a deeper experience in their knowledge of God. This week let's examine a few people who had their faith in God interrupted. Read Genesis 39:1-23.

Joseph's life seemed to be rolling right along. He moved up the corporate ladder in the house of Potiphar. He received a promotion because of his diligence at work. Life was good until GFI occurred.

Answer the questions below to trace what happened to Joseph.
List three facts we discover in verse 2 about Joseph.

_____

_____

_____

Which of these three tidbits of information do you consider most important?

_____

What was Joseph put in charge of in verse 6? How is he described in this verse?

_____

_____

Scripture describes Joseph as well-built and handsome. Not only a hunk of man, but he held a position of power. But most important, we read, "The Lord was with Joseph" (verse 2). His faith in God probably was never stronger—life was good. However, in verse 6 we also read of the initial GFI that tripped up Joseph's life.

81

How then could I do such a wicked thing and sin against God? Genesis 39:9b

What did Potiphar's wife do? She took notice of Joseph. A lustful current swept her off her feet. She desired Joseph and declared her intent.

Write down the various reasons Joseph refused her.

_____

_____

Briefly describe what took place in verses 10-18.

_____

How did Potiphar react in verse 19?

_____

Faith Fiction
When the Lord is with us nothing bad ever occurs.

Joseph behaved as a godly man. Although he was a young virile man, Joseph fled from the temptation of adultery. Why? Because he would not betray his earthly master, nor sin against the God he loved and trusted. But still, a God Faith Interrupter occurred and Joseph landed in prison. Scripture does not state whether or not Joseph stumbled in faith, but his circumstance certainly held the possibility of a GFI.

If you were Joseph, what emotions would you have experienced?

_____

What questions would have raced through your mind?

_____

_____

Fill in the blanks in the verses below. "Joseph's master took him and put him in prison, the place where the king's prisoners were confined. _____ while Joseph was there in the _____, the _____ was with him; _____ showed him _____ and granted him favor in the eyes of the prison warden" (Genesis 39:20, 21).
Well, well . . . the Lord was with Joseph. I wonder if Joseph recognized this or if he felt totally alone?

Can you describe a time when you felt alone, but later knew God had been with you?

_____

How do you know *now* the Lord was with you?

_____

_____

Read Genesis 39:21 from the *Amplified Bible*.

During the GIF, did He display mercy and loving-kindness? If yes, describe how you experienced it.

_____

But the Lord was with Joseph, and showed him mercy and loving-kindness and gave him favor in the sight of the warden of the prison. Genesis 39:21, AMP

In the verses below, underline the phrase that could have applied to Joseph's experiences and feelings while in a dark prison.

Be strong and courageous, do not be afraid or tremble at them, for the LORD your God is the one who goes with you. He will not fail you or forsake you. Deuteronomy 31:6, NASB

Have mercy on me, O God, have mercy on me, for in you my soul takes refuge. I will take refuge in the shadow of your wings until the disaster has passed. Psalm 57:1

The LORD appeared to us in the past, saying: "I have loved you with an everlasting love; I have drawn you with loving-kindness." Jeremiah 31:3

Bearing fruit in every good work, growing in the knowledge of God, being strengthened with all power according to his glorious might so that you may have great endurance and patience, and joyfully giving thanks to the Father. Colossians 1:10-12b

It's certainly difficult to understand the twists and turns in our journey of faith. When a God Faith Interrupter occurs, we need to grope in the darkness for verses to assure us that regardless of our circumstance, the Lord is loving, merciful, and

Faith Fact
God's love, mercy, guidance, and presence are always with us.

He will guide us. God Faith Interrupters might shake faith. They will be scary. They certainly will be unexpected and uncomfortable, but the Lord holds the charge of power to uplift our faith even when it shuts down temporarily. James Dobson says,

> If we truly understood the majesty of this Lord and the depth of His love for us, we would certainly accept those times when He defies human logic and sensibilities. Indeed that is what we *must* do. Expect confusing experiences to occur along the way. Welcome them as friends—as opportunities for your faith to grow.[1]

Express to the Lord your fear of a God Faith Interrupter. Then thank Him that He will be with you, showing you mercy and lovingkindness, no matter what happens in this life.

Faith Fun
Read Genesis 37:1-36, 39:1-23, 40:1-23; and 41:1-40. Then place an X in the margin of your Bible every time the phrase "the Lord was with Joseph and gave him success in whatever he did" (Genesis 39:23) would have aptly applied to Joseph and his circumstances.

Lord,

In Jesus' name, I pray. Amen

Faith Finale!

But while Joseph was there in the prison, the Lord was with him; he showed him kindness and granted him favor in the eyes of the prison warden. Genesis 39:20, 21

Day 2 – **Bootleg Faith**

Lord,

Forgive me for not taking ownership of my faith. Enable me to depend on You alone for my faith, not to others who impress me with their religiosity. Show me how to make my faith my own.

In Jesus' name, Amen

A skeleton hangs in my family history closet. It's very quiet. No one brings the skeleton to our family gatherings. It seldom rattles, but when it does, we all look at each other appalled. *How can our family have a history of bootlegging?*
To my shock and dismay, it's true. My great-grandfather and grandpa bootlegged alcohol during the Prohibition of the 1920s. The original term, *bootleg*, comes from the attempt to conceal something, usually whiskey, in a flask down the inside of a high-top boot. However, during the Prohibition, the word *bootleg* was soon coined to mean brewing drink that was only a copy of the real thing— whiskey.

So, when the government prohibited the making or selling of any type of alcohol, my forefathers saw opportunity. They contrived a small distillery in a basement and sold the liquid gold at exorbitant prices. The folk who remember the brew said it smelled like oil and tasted like acid. However, it was in high demand. So, the "family wealth" expanded from the illegal activity of making something that produced the desired effect—drunkenness—but no one actually considered the concoction the "real stuff." The bootlegged moonshine made everyone happy—my ancestors and the city drunks.

Sometimes our faith is bootlegged. We tuck their "faith" inside our spirit, so we can be "spiritual." Or, like my "family wealth," perhaps our faith is passed down to us. We assume it's real. "Family faith" feels comfortable, like a well-worn leather boot. We participate in all sorts of rituals, celebrations, and prayers that we don't understand or even care about. Bootlegged faith is never authentic growing faith. It's fake faith.

Today, we'll examine three examples of bootlegged faith in the Bible. Let's learn how we can make faith our own, not a bootlegged copy of someone else's.
Read Acts 8:9-24, 1 Samuel 13:7b-14, and 1 Samuel 30, 31.

What do you find similar in what Simon (Acts 8:24) and Saul (1 Samuel 15:30) said?

_____

_____

Faith Fiction
We can garner faith
through another's faith.

Has there ever been a time when you did not want to pray yourself, but asked someone else to pray for you? If yes, why? What was the outcome?

_____

Take a moment and consider the results of prayer if:
- You pray for yourself, but ask no one else to pray.
- You ask someone to pray, but then neglect to pray for yourself.
- You pray for yourself, but, in addition, share your prayer request with someone you trust.

For where two or three come together in my name, there am I with them.
Matthew 18:20

In the margin read Matthew 18:20. What promise did Jesus give?

_____

How does Matthew 18:20 encourage you to pray with and for others?

_____

For myself, I have found that when I pray and ask other believers to pray with me, I experience greater results. Not only do I usually see more specific answers, but also I have someone else to encourage me to pray when I am discouraged, especially when I haven't yet seen any answers.

My prayer partner, Shelley, and I pray most Mondays. We have done this for several years. We pray specifically for our children. Over the years, our prayer journals have become filled with requests. Some requests are answered quickly. Other prayers are still waiting for God's response, but our hope remains steady. My heart waits in peace, when I realize that Christ is with us as we huddle over the kitchen table, lifting our children in prayer to the throne room of God. Let's read another passage of Scripture that correlates to Matthew 18:20. Please read Hebrews 4:14-16. How does this passage speak to us about the possibility of "bootlegging faith" from someone else?

_____

Whom does Jesus represent as high priest?

_____

How are we to hold on to our faith?

_____

Why does Jesus have the ability to sympathize with us?

_____

Let's speculate about Simon and Saul. How do you think things might have turned out if they had prayed to God on their own in accordance with Hebrews 4:16?

_____

For Saul?

_____

For Simon?

_____

So let us come boldly to the throne of our gracious God. There we will receive his mercy, and we will find grace to help us when we need it most.
Hebrews 4:16, NLT

Of course, we will never know, but perhaps they would have become mighty men of God. If only Simon and Saul had fallen on their knees to pray for themselves and asked others to pray *with* them, not just *for* them. I believe their stories would have ended quite differently.

Our faith must be our own. We can't depend on anyone else to grow faith for us. However, we can look to others for help, guidance, and counseling. Let's read about Ruth. She was a woman who accepted God as her own God, yet learned to exercise faith based on another godly woman's faith—Naomi, her mother-in-law. Read Ruth 1:1-18. Briefly describe the circumstances of Naomi, Orpah, and Ruth.

_____

What did Orpah decide to do?

_____

Faith Fact
Spiritual growth occurs, through the power of God, and our commitments to pursue an intimate relationship with Jesus Christ.

87

How did Ruth respond to Naomi's urging to return home?

_____

Reread verse 17. What indication does this verse give that Ruth possessed her *own* faith in Naomi's God?

_____

Three widows were alone in a land experiencing famine. Naomi decided to return to her home in Judah. Orpah kissed Naomi good-bye and left. However, Ruth chose to follow Naomi. Her words, "May the LORD deal with me, be it ever so severely, if anything but death separates you and me" (verse 17), displayed her faith. She spoke as a woman who knew the Lord God from her own experience, not just from Naomi's teaching on God.

Read 1 Peter 3:15. How does this verse relate to our lesson that our faith cannot be bootlegged, but it must be our own?

_____

How would this apply to Ruth?

_____

Are you able to give an answer for your belief in Jesus?

_____

In closing, read the genealogy of Jesus Christ in Matthew 1:1-16. What do we discover in verse 5?

_____

Yes, Ruth's faith found its way down through the centuries. Her faith, by using Naomi as a godly example, resulted in Ruth being listed in the genealogy of our Jesus. I don't know about you, but this makes me want to pursue my personal faith more diligently.

Close today with a prayer asking God to help us not to "bootleg" faith from any source. Ask Him to grant us the same intensity of faith as Ruth possessed.

Lord God,

In Jesus' name, Amen

Faith Fun
Unscramble the people's names found in today's lesson.
hutr
lasu
mniso
lemusa
debo
imona
treep
arpoh

Faith Finale!

But in your hearts set apart Christ as Lord. Always be prepared to give an answer to everyone who asks you to give the reason for the hope that you have. 1 Peter 3:15

Day 3 – **Prophets in the Pits**

Lord Jesus.

Help me to keep my face and my faith lifted up toward You. Teach me to walk in obedience, even when it's hard.

In Your name, Amen

I woke up in the pits of life today. Nothing special happened to cause my blues. It was just the garden varieties of life the day before: a spat with my husband, household bills, the dog threw up, and a pile of laundry. I crawled out of bed and slipped down the blue slide of depression, hitting the pits of life.

I rationalize that if I do everything I am "supposed" to do, then life will be glorious. If I read my Bible, pray, and go to church, doesn't it make sense that my life should be joy-filled? However, God's design for a day-to-day, faith-filled life differs from our human expectation.

Since you probably wake up occasionally in the same state of mind as I did, let's study a few people who had great faith, but experienced the pits of life too.

Today's lesson contains examples of people who found themselves in the pits. We are going to study three prophets of God—Jeremiah, Ezekiel, and Hosea. These men held the position and title of prophets of God. Prophets were spokespersons for God. Sometimes the Lord foretold impending disaster and other times promises of hope through them. Let's see where their life of obedient faith landed them.

Read Jeremiah 38:1-13. Mark a T for True or an F for False next to the following statements concerning Jeremiah.

_____ He spoke what God said.
_____ The city would be rescued.
_____ The officials followed Jeremiah's advice.
_____ The King agreed with Jeremiah.
_____ Jeremiah was thrown into a mud-filled cistern.
_____ Jeremiah was pulled out.
_____ Jeremiah was free to go anywhere.

Read Jeremiah 40:1-6. Describe briefly the next events in Jeremiah's life. Where was Jeremiah still?

_____

What happened to Judah?

_____

What did the commander of the guard offer to Jeremiah?

_____

What did Jeremiah choose to do in verse 6?

_____

I can honestly say I probably would have taken the commander of the guard's offer. Freedom in Babylon over devastation in Judah would have sounded very appealing. Yet, Jeremiah chose to stay and wait out the disaster with His Lord God. He trusted God's hand even after a muddy cistern, a courtyard prison, and the destruction of Judah.

Why would Jeremiah decide to wait in Jerusalem? Let's find out. Read the following verses and note what you discover.

Jeremiah 32:1, 2 _____

Jeremiah 32:6-9 _____

Jeremiah 32:26-29 _____

Jeremiah 32:37-41 _____

Although Jeremiah knew Babylon would destroy the city, he also knew what God had promised. The Lord God promised to restore the fortunes of Israel. He would bring them back to their homeland to prosper them. Jeremiah's faith weathered the muddy cistern—a pit in life.

Now let's read about the prophet Ezekiel. He, too, experienced the harsh reality of life as a committed follower of an unexplainable God.

Read the following verses and note what your feelings would have been if you were Ezekiel.

Ezekiel 2:5-8
Your thoughts and feelings?_____

Ezekiel 4:4, 5
Your thoughts and feelings?_____

Ezekiel 5:1-4
Your thoughts and feelings?_____

Ezekiel 24:15-18
Your thoughts and feelings?_____

God's commands and Ezekiel's obedience are quite strange, don't you agree? I can't explain them, but the *Holman's Bible Dictionary*, provides us with an easy to understand and concise explanation:

> Much has been written about Ezekiel's personality. He has been labeled neurotic, paranoid, psychotic, or schizophrenic because of his unusual behavior (for example, lying on one side for 390 days and on the other for 40 days, Ezekiel 4:4-6; shaving off his hair, Ezekiel 5:1-4; and his many visions). A better explanation for his

strange behavior is that anyone who conscientiously obeys God will be considered "strange" by some people. Nothing God asked Ezekiel to do seemed too difficult. Only once was he reluctant to obey a command that would have made him ceremonially unclean (Ezekiel 4:14). His objection reflected his priestly training. [2]

Obedience to God doesn't always make sense. Nor are we promised a life that will only be pleasant and filled with joyful experiences.

We are going to read one more example of a prophet of God—Hosea. God requested something that appears out of character for both God and Hosea. Let's see what it was and write down the obedient acts of Hosea.

Hosea 1:2, 3: _____

Hosea 3:1-4: _____

Oh, my! Another one that is so hard to explain. Again, I fall back on scholars who have more knowledge than I do. Read the following explanations of God's request and Hosea's obedience,

> Many have questioned why God would tell Hosea to marry a wife who would be unfaithful to him, but it must be understood that God intended to use this marriage as an illustration of His dealings with Israel. God used Gomer's adultery to expose Israel's sin because it vividly reflected Israel's unfaithfulness. Hosea bought back his adulterous wife, illustrating the fact that God would redeem His estranged people. [3]

After reading about Jeremiah, Ezekiel, and Hosea, my blues don't seem hard at all. Actually, I feel quite light-hearted and ready to tackle the mountain of laundry in the hallway. How about you?

_____

How does your life compare to the prophets in the pits?

_____

Jeremiah, Ezekiel, and Hosea chose to follow the Lord God even when it wasn't going to be a fun-filled day. I believe each of them would remind us to recite Psalm

3:3 when we fall into the pits of life. "But You, O LORD, are a shield about me, My glory, and the One who lifts my head" (Psalm 3:3, NASB).

No matter how far down the slippery slide of depression and doubt we slide, God is the shield about us and the lifter of our heads. Can you hear the distant echo of Jeremiah, Ezekiel and Hosea shouting a hearty, "Hallelujah, Amen!"?

But You, O Lord,

Faith Fun
Find a children's Bible and read the stories of Jeremiah, Ezekiel, and Hosea. Write a short poem from each of the prophet's point of view.

In Jesus' name, Amen

Faith Finale!
But Thou, O Lord, art a shield about me, My glory, and the One who lifts my head.
Psalm 3:3, NASB

Day 4 – **Whispers of Why**

Lord God,

Sometimes You do not make sense to me. Today a sorrow scorches my heart. I want to know why bad things happen to people I love. Grant me the peace that comes with knowing You are a good God. Soothe my heart. Help me accept that Your will is not always understandable on this side of eternity.

In Jesus' name, Amen

"You have cancer—stage four lung cancer. I would begin to get your household in order," said the oncologist.

My dear friend called and told me the doctor's report. I heard her weeping. Then through muffled sobs she asked, "How can this be? I am only 44. I have never smoked. Why me?"

I sat stunned, thinking back over the past few months. There had been no warning of the devastating illness—just a small pain in her upper back. We assumed she had tweaked her back. We laughed about how painful an "ergonomical" chair could turn out to be. Now this.

"I don't know why," I said with a voice hardly above a whisper.

Yesterday we studied about the prophets and could see God's hand in the reason they landed in the pits of life. But today, we are going to search Scripture to look for the "whys" that God doesn't explain to us. He wants us to trust Him when our whispered "whys" scream from our soul to heaven, "WHY?"

We will not find answers or conclusions to our "whys", but I pray we will find solace, comfort, and peace as we allow our faith to rest in God's sovereignty. Read the following Scriptures and then match the reference to the correct event.

Acts 7:54—8:1	Peter miraculously rescued from Herod's prison
Acts 12:1, 2	Paul stoned, left for dead, but lived
Acts 12:3	James killed by Herod in prison
Acts 12:6-11	Stephen stoned to death
Acts 14:19, 20	Peter placed in prison by Herod

Why was James killed, but Peter miraculously released from Herod's grip? Why did God allow Stephen to be stoned to death by an angry mob? How come Paul walked away from the pile of stones thrown by an angry mob? We don't know.

We are not alone in our question of "why." People of the Christian faith often experience periods of doubt about the goodness of God and His will. I pray this lesson will help ease our painful confusion. How does the Bible direct us in our "whispers of why"?

_____

First, read 1 Samuel 13:14 and Acts 13:22. What do both of these verses tell us about David?

_____

How would you define the phrase, "a man after His own heart?"

_____

What does Acts 13:22 imply to you about David and his faith?

_____

Do you consider yourself a woman after God's own heart? Why or why not?

_____

We will look at David and his attitude about the sovereign hand of God in his life by reading three stories about David and his "why" circumstances. Answer the following questions and then jot down how you might have responded in the same situations.

Read 1 Samuel 18:3, 4; 20:41, 42; 2 Samuel 1:17; 25, 26; 2:1 Describe the relationship between Jonathan and David.

_____

What happened to Jonathan?

_____

What emotions did David display?

_____

How did David respond?

_____

What would be your response?

_____

Read 2 Samuel 12:15-23. What did David do in verse 16?

_____

What happened to the child in verse 18?

_____

What emotion did David display?

_____

How did David respond in verse 20a?

_____

What would have been your response?

_____

Read 2 Samuel 15:14, 30; 16:5-14.
What news did David receive? (2 Samuel 15:14)

_____

What emotion did David display? (2 Samuel 15:30)

_____

What did Shimei say to David?

_____

How did David respond to the curse? (verse 10)

_____

Who was David fleeing from and what was his response? (2 Samuel 16:11, 12)

_____

What would have been your response?

_____

David lost his best friend and his newborn son. For a time, David lost his kingdom to Absalom, the son who mutinied against him. Each time David grieved. He allowed his emotions to vent. However, at the same time he grieved, he rested in the Lord's sovereignty in his life. David refused to believe anything other than that God knew best about the details of his life, details David could not understand himself.

Although David does not ask, "Why?" many times the question is asked in the Bible.

Read the following verses from Psalms. Note what the "why" is and how the author of the psalm responded to his own question.

Psalm 2:1, 4-6
The why: _____

The answer: _____

Psalm 3:1-8
The why: _____

The answer: _____

Psalm 10:1; 17, 18
The why: _____

The answer: _____

Psalm 22:1, 2; 24
The why: _____

The answer: _____

Psalm 42:5
The why: _____

The answer: _____

The psalmists questioned why, but also acknowledged that the Lord is a good and faithful God whether or not His ways can be understood. Read the following psalms and underline the phrase that contains the word *good*.

Faith Fact
Scripture assures us that God is good.

97

I am still confident of this: I will see the goodness of the LORD in the land of the living. Psalm 27:13

You are forgiving and good, O Lord, abounding in love to all who call to you. Psalm 86:5 *For the Lord is good and his love endures forever; his faithfulness continues through all generations.* Psalm 100:5

The Lord is good to all; he has compassion on all he has made. Psalm 145:9

What can we learn from the psalmists? How can we fall back on these nuggets of truth when our own world falls apart? How can my friend begin to cope with her devastating news of terminal cancer? Is it all right to whisper whys? Is it okay to question God?

We certainly will have our "whys" while we are here on earth. It is all right to ask our question, but there's a likely probability that God will not answer to our satisfaction. I would like us to consider author James Dobson's words:

> God usually does not choose to answer those questions in this life! . . . He will not parade His plans and purposes for our approval. We must never forget that He is God. He wants us to believe and trust Him despite the things we don't understand . . . . We are relieved from the responsibility of trying to figure them out. We haven't been given enough information to decipher the code. It is enough to acknowledge that God makes sense when He doesn't make sense.[4]

Close today's lesson with acknowledging that we cannot begin to fathom God's ways in our life or the world at large. Read the following verses and apply them to your own lack of understanding and questions.

For My thoughts are not your thoughts, Nor are your ways My ways, declares the LORD. Isaiah 55:9

It is God who arms me with strength and makes my way perfect. Psalm 18:32

Danger may lurk ahead. But God is good. We must trust His goodness when our "whispers of why" go unanswered.

My Jesus, my King,

Faith Fun
Read *The Lion, the Witch, and the Wardrobe* by C.S. Lewis (or rent the DVD). As you read or watch it, place yourself in Lucy's shoes. Note all the different "whys" she might be asking throughout the entire story.

In Your name, Amen

Faith Finale!
I am still confident of this: I will see the goodness of the LORD in the land of the living. Psalm 27:13

Day 5 – **Faith Failure**

Lord Jesus,

I have failed You in the past. My faith shattered. I know You have forgiven me, but it's hard for me to forgive myself. Today help me to see that my failed faith can be used as a step to grow into a deeper intimacy with You.

In Your name, I pray. Amen

I failed my faith test. I strode away from God in anger, frustration, and doubt. He didn't "behave" the way I requested. My prayers weren't answered, in fact, I felt like they were ignored. So, when I was in my early twenties, I threw a spiritual temper tantrum. One day I stood in my kitchen, looked up at the heavens and declared, "I will do it on my own then!" My snit at God lasted for several years. My immature faith failed. Thankfully, God didn't give up on me. He allowed me to wander away, but He wooed me back into fellowship with Himself. Although my faith was once again growing and maturing, I struggled to get over the regret of my failure. Guilt plagued me when I prayed, went to church, or studied the Bible. "What kind of Christian am I? How could I have walked away from the Lord I love? I am a fraud and a failure."

My friend, can you relate? We all fail in our faith. It might not be on as large a scale as mine was, but it's a stumble in the growth of our faith. Once we make a mistake in discipleship with the Lord, the devil uses our failure to thwart future faith growth. Satan shadows us and reminds us of our colossal crash. He haunts our efforts to be effective Christians with accusations of fraud. "You fraud! You are a failure!"

Thankfully, we can move beyond our faith failures and use them as fertilizer to produce mustard seeds of faith. Today, the Scriptures will cheer us on to a deeper faith. So, my friend, let's discover the truth about our past (and future) failures of faith.

Read Luke 9:20. What did Peter declare?

_____

Read Luke 22:31-34. Fill in the blanks of these verses.
Verse 32: "Simon, that your faith may not fail. And when you _____ _____ back,_____ your brothers."
Verse 33: "But he replied, 'Lord, _____ _____ _____ to go with you to _____ and to _____.'"
Verse 34: "Jesus answered, 'I tell you, Peter, before the rooster crows today, _____will _____ three times that _____ _____ _____.'"

Read Luke 22:54-62. What did Jesus do in verse 61?

_____

How did Peter respond in verse 62?

_____

Jesus knew Simon Peter much better than Simon Peter knew himself. Peter believed his faith was strong enough to be imprisoned and even to die for Jesus. However, Jesus foretold that Peter would deny Him three times that night. And that's exactly what Peter did. As soon as the rooster crowed, Jesus turned and

Faith Fiction
Our faith will never stumble or fail.

looked at Peter. Can you imagine what went through the minds of both Jesus and Peter? The phrase, "looked straight at" comes from the Greek word *emblép*. It means, to look in the face, fix the eyes upon, in the sense of to look at or upon, meaning to contemplate.[5]   Jesus gazed deep into the soul of Peter. Peter's surety of faith crashed into the abyss of sorrow. Luke 22:62 tells us Peter wept bitterly. The Greek definition of "wept bitterly" grants us a much clearer picture of Peter's reaction to his faith failure. The phrase means wail and lament. It implies not only the shedding of tears, but also displaying every external expression of grief—the grief of bitterness that feels cruel and harsh.[6]

I relate so closely to these passages in the Bible. I, too, thought I loved Jesus enough to die for Him. But when the going became tough, I walked away in anger. However, my mutiny did not come as a surprise to Jesus, any more than Peter's denial. Jesus knew. He told Peter, "when you have turned back, strengthen your brothers" (verse 32). The same is true for all of us.

Read the rest of Peter's story. Read John 21:15-17 and Acts 2:14-41.
After the resurrection, Jesus forgave and encouraged Peter. I imagine Peter jumped up, whooped and hollered, and then collapsed in tears before the nail-scarred feet in complete humility and gratitude. After that, Peter chose to prove his faith to a multitude of people—very persuasively, too, I might add.

How and why are we able to strengthen others after we stumble in our faith?

_____

_____

Faith Fact
God uses our worst failures to produce some of our greatest victories.

Once we realize the frailty of our faith, we can humbly share our own faith mishaps with others who are struggling. God will receive the glory for His love, mercy, and grace in the restoration of our faith. Others will witness God's faithfulness, regardless of our failures, and be encouraged to continue in their own walk.

However, we still must deal with the self-imposed guilt of our failure. Do you think Peter was ever haunted by his denial of Christ? Why or why not?

_____

_____

101

Read the following verses written by Peter. Note how they could apply to Peter and to yourself during a failure of faith.

_____

_____

These have come so that your faith—of greater worth than gold, which perishes even though refined by fire—may be proved genuine and may result in praise, glory and honor when Jesus Christ is revealed. 1 Peter 1:7

Peter: _____

You: _____

Be self-controlled and alert. Your enemy the devil prowls around like a roaring lion looking for someone to devour. 1 Peter 5:8

Peter: _____

You: _____

But in your hearts set apart Christ as Lord. Always be prepared to give an answer to everyone who asks you to give the reason for the hope that you have. But do this with gentleness and respect. 1 Peter 3:15

Peter: _____

You: _____

Close this week's lessons with a prayer. Then complete Faith Seed Thoughts & Prayers.

Faith Fact
God can use our worst failures to produce some of our greatest victories.

Faith Finale!
These have come so that your faith—of greater worth than gold, which perishes even though refined by fire—may be proved genuine and may result in praise, glory and honor when Jesus Christ is revealed. 1 Peter 1:7

Faith Seed Thoughts & Prayers – **Review Week 4**
Journal your thoughts about how this week's lessons applied to you personally.

Faith Fun
Read the fiction book, *The Screwtape Letters* by C.S. Lewis. As you read consider why we become "faith heroes" or "faith failures."

1 Dobson, James. *When God Doesn't Make Sense*, (Wheaton, IL: Tyndale House Publishers, Inc.), 1993. p. 69.

2 *Holman Bible Dictionary*. Copyright c 1991 Holman Bible Publishers. Used by special arrangement with Broadman & Holman Publishers. Database c NavPress Software.

3 Zodhiates, Spiros, Th.D. Exe. Ed & Baker, Warren, *Hebrew-Greek Study Bible*, (Chattanooga, TN: AMG Publishers, 1996), p. 1043, 1045.

4 Dobson, James. *When God Doesn't Make Sense*, (Wheaton, IL: Tyndale House Publishers, Inc.), 1993. p. 236-238.

5 Zodhiates, Spiros, Th.D., The *Complete Word Study Dictionary: New Testament*, (Chattanooga, TN: AMG Publishers) 1992. #1689 p. 573.

6 Ibid. #2799, p. 864; #4089, p. 1158.

Week 5
Resting in the Shade

Day 1 – **A Celebration of Faith**

Heavenly Father,

I confess that I do not rest as I should. I do not spend time alone with You without my to-do list rattling around in my thoughts. I do not take time to enjoy and celebrate my relationship with You. Lord, help me to commit to more time of rest and relaxation. Teach me to celebrate my faith.

In Jesus' name, Amen

As I write today, the brilliant colored leaves sway in the chilly breeze. The leaves fall gently to the ground and then crunch as my dogs paw at them. The brisk weather and array of colors remind me of the majesty of God. His creation reveals His glory and it blesses me deep within my soul. It's November.

Thanksgiving Day is approaching quickly and I need to plan the menu and go grocery shopping. Thanksgiving is a time to recognize the bounty of blessings we usually take for granted. It's a day to acknowledge God's goodness and truly thank Him for the magnificent minutiae that meander through our day-to-day lives. Of course, I use this holiday as a time to encourage my children to be thankful for God's goodness we have experienced throughout the year.

However, for me, Thanksgiving turns out to be a day of work. I cook, clean, and grumble. At the end of the day, I tumble onto the couch exhausted. I admit I do not know how to rest and celebrate even a day of thanksgiving to the God I adore. Today we are going to look at God's perspective on work, rest, and celebration. I think we will be pleasantly surprised by God's opinion of rest and celebration, since it contrasts starkly to our activity-driven culture.

Read the verses below and write what you discover about God from each of the verses.

Genesis 1:31 _____

Genesis 2:1-3 _____

Genesis 2:9 _____

What do these verses teach us about why God rested?

_____

_____

Because God is God, He didn't have to rest because He had over exerted Himself. Let's think about it for a moment. We read, "God saw all that he had made, and it was very good" (1:31). In verse 2:9, we saw that God's new creation was "pleasing to the eye and good for food". Hmmm . . . perhaps He reveled in the result of His creation. Maybe God rested to *enjoy* the fruit of His labor. (No pun intended.) Sunday is usually considered the Sabbath in our culture. Years ago, all stores were closed on Sundays. People went to church and usually came home to a large home-cooked meal. Sunday was a day to honor God and to rest for the upcoming workweek.

Faith Fiction
We should never celebrate our faith accomplishments.

Describe your Sunday activities.

_____

_____

Look at the original Hebrew word for rested—*ša<u>b</u>at*. The original definition includes the ideas to rest, to cease, to come to an end, to keep or celebrate the Sabbath.[1]

How often do you rest and enjoy the fruit of your labor? Explain your answer.

_____

_____

List five ways in which we might be able to celebrate our "work."

1. _____

2. _____

3. _____

4. _____

5. _____

Do you find contentment in the results of your work or do you have a nagging feeling it could have been better? Explain why you have these feelings and thoughts.

_____

_____

I often think after I have finished a task, "It could have been better. I should have tried harder." Satisfaction and contentment elude me. I find this true in my faith journey too.

I believe if I try harder, my faith will be deeper, more complete, and please God more.

Do you hold these same thoughts and feelings about your journey of faith? If yes, why?

God wants us to celebrate our faith. Even if it is as small as a mustard seed, we should rejoice—not because of our faith, but because of who God is in our lives. Our faith journey will never be complete, but it is something to celebrate.

Underline the phrase of rejoicing found in the following verses.

I will be glad and rejoice in you; I will sing praise to your name, O Most High.
  Psalm 9:2

Rejoice in the Lord and be glad, you righteous; sing, all you who are upright in heart!
Psalm 32:11

 In him our hearts rejoice, for we trust in his holy name.   Psalm 33:21

But may all who seek you rejoice and be glad in you; may those who love your salvation always say, "The LORD be exalted." Psalm 40:16a

Let's discover what God says about celebrating and rejoicing in Him.
Read the following Scriptures that were given to the Hebrew people as instructions to celebrate the Lord God, then note what thoughts stand out to you.

Exodus 12:14 _____

Exodus 23:14-16 _____

Deuteronomy 16:15 _____

As I ponder these verses, these concepts come to my mind. We need to celebrate special faith occasions with our families, especially our children. Of course, we celebrate Christmas and Easter, but I think we need to move a step beyond the usual religious holidays. Perhaps we could celebrate the anniversary of our baptism, or we might throw a party when we have memorized ten Scripture verses. If we want to make our faith visible to our children and grandchildren, we must celebrate our faith achievements in ways that will be memorable, not only to ourselves, but to them.

The verses in Exodus, if applied today, would urge us to celebrate often. They would encourage us to rejoice when we plant a seed of faith and to celebrate when our harvest of faith comes in. Sounds like fun, doesn't it?

Read Nehemiah 8:9, 10, 12 and 12:27, 28. Apply these verses to our modern culture. What could we do that would be similar?

Faith Fact
God designed times of celebration and spiritual renewal.

_____

_____

Faith Fun
Choose a Sunday to celebrate the week's accomplishments. In addition, either with family or friends (or both), plan a day to celebrate your faith. Rejoice in the Lord! Allow it to be a time without a lot of fuss, but fun. Rejoice with others that your faith is growing and that, "it is very good."

Note a few ideas on how and when we could celebrate our faith.

_____

_____

Faith Finale!

So the people went away to eat a festive meal, to share gifts of food, and to celebrate with great joy because they had heard God's words and understood them.
Nehemiah 8:12, NLT

Day 2 – **A God Who Naps**

Father God,

Remind me that sleep is important. Help me to realize that sleep not only aids my physical and mental state, but that a lack of sleep becomes a detriment to my faith. Lord, I want my faith to grow strong and that means I need to make sleep a priority.

In Jesus' name, Amen

Faith Fiction
Sleep is a waste of time.

Because in our culture we feel we need to make more money, possess the latest gadget, and provide every want of our children, we deprive ourselves of necessary sleep to obtain more "work" hours in the day. Most people need at least seven to eight hours of sleep a night. (I function best with nine hours of sleep.) However, the American Medical Association estimates that between 50 to 70 million people function, on a daily basis, without adequate sleep. The popular assumption is that sleep is a waste of precious time, but the side effects due to the lack of sleep include fatigue, exhaustion, anxiety, stress, irritability, depression, and weight gain.[2] I relate to all of the side effects. (But, I suppose it's a great excuse for my weight gain.)

Can you relate? If yes, explain why you experience a lack of sleep.

_____

Place an X next to the side effect(s) you experience and then note how often you experience them.

___ Fatigue   ___ Exhaustion   ___ Anxiety   ___ Stress

___ Irritability   ___ Depression   ___ Weight gain

God created sleep. At the beginning of creation, He created our bodies to need slumber. Let's examine what the Bible tells us about sleep and our need for it. When sleeping is first mentioned? Read Genesis 2:21.

Who slept? _____

In your opinion, why did God cause Adam to fall into a deep sleep?

_____

Sleep promotes healing of the physical body. It reduces or eliminates pain. Sleep allows the body's natural healing mechanisms to work without interference. Sleep is needed to regenerate our bodies as well as our mental health. Let's look at an example of this principle.

Read Matthew 26:36-43. Jesus wanted the disciples to stay awake to watch and pray with Him. But each time He returned to them, He found them in deep slumber. I find this interesting. It seems that if Christ asked them to pray, they should have huddled together for a mighty prayer session. However, they just couldn't seem to keep their faith awake to pray.

Read the same account in the other gospels to discover more about what caused the disciples' inability to stay awake. Read Luke 22:39-46.

What reason is given for their chronic tiredness? (verse 45)

_____

Read Mark 14:32-42.

How did the disciples respond to Jesus' question? (verse 40)

_____

I suffer from arthritis in my neck. The best remedy for my pain is to sleep with a warm towel pressed against my neck. And when I feel sad—I want to sleep. On a day when depression stalks my thoughts, I just want to stay in bed with the covers pulled over my head. The act of sleep helps the mind cope with pain, both physical and emotional. Can you list a time when either physical or mental suffering occurred and sleep helped you cope?

Without warning, a furious storm came up on the lake, so that the waves swept over the boat. But Jesus was sleeping.
Matthew 8:24

_____

Sleep holds the ability to restore our strength physically, emotionally, and spiritually. Even Jesus, as a human being, needed to sleep and restore Himself. Read the following verses and note what Jesus is doing.

Matthew 8:23, 24 _____

Faith Fact
God created sleep to restore our bodies, minds, and spirits.

Mark 4:35-38 _____

Read Matthew 8:16, 18.
What was Jesus doing before He took a nap?

_____

What caused Jesus to give orders to cross to the other side of the lake?

_____

Ministering to people caused Jesus to seek a nap. I can relate. I served as a women's ministries director at my church for several years. Our church held three services on Sunday mornings, and every Sunday afternoon, I collapsed in my bed for a long restful nap. Caring for others strains the resources of our human bodies, and Jesus was not an exception. While He walked on earth, His body required sleep. If Jesus needed to nap, I believe it is permissible for us to doze off occasionally too.

Check any boxes that apply to the people you care for on a regular basis.

☐ Children   ☐ Co-workers   ☐ Husband   ☐ Church ministries   ☐ Parents
☐ Neighbors   ☐ Friends   ☐ Community

What types of naps do you take? Mark an X on the line below to specify your naps.

_____

Naps are a waste of time   10 minute power naps   30 minute catnaps   1 hour sleep   2 hours + deep sleep

God created our bodies and minds to refresh themselves while we sleep. Although we may feel we do not have time to sleep, the truth is we don't have time *not* to sleep. But sleep is God's gift to us. Psalm 127:2 says, "He grants sleep to those he loves." Even Shakespeare wrote about the benefits of sleep in Macbeth.

> Sleep that knits up the ravelled sleave of care,
>
> The death of each day's life, sore labour's bath,
>
> Balm of hurt minds, great Nature's second course,
>
> Chief nourisher in life's feast. (Act II, Scene II)

Ponder this stanza. Can you paraphrase it in modern English?

_____

_____

Scripture encourages us to sleep (in the example of Jesus napping) and assures us God protects us while we sleep. Read the following verses and note what they promise. Then fill in the blanks with your name.

"_____ lies down and sleeps; _____ wakes again, because the LORD sustains her" (Psalm 3:5).

"_____ will lie down and sleep in peace, for you alone, O LORD, make her dwell in safety" (Psalm 4:8).

"When _____ lies down, she will not be afraid; when _____ lies down, her sleep will be sweet" (Proverbs 3:24).

If you have trouble sleeping, memorize theses verse or write them on index cards that you keep next to your bed. I pray that they comfort you as you sleep in God's presence.

He will not let your foot slip—he who watches over you will not slumber; indeed, he who watches over Israel will neither slumber nor sleep.
Psalm 121:3, 4

111

Close today with one final thought. We read that Jesus, in His human body, required sleep. He napped. However, do not worry about our God sleeping during a crisis in your life. He sits on the throne of heaven watching while *you* slumber. Read Psalm 121:3, 4. What does it state about our God and sleep?

Faith Fun

Take a nap at least once this week.

_____

God never sleeps! He watches over us as our human bodies drift off into slumber. So, we've learned today we must allow ourselves enough sleep and rest. Our faith will be able to bloom if we take care of our physical bodies. Jesus napped—so can we!

Faith Finale!
You'll take afternoon naps without a worry, you'll enjoy a good night's sleep.
Proverbs 3:24, MSG

Day 3 – **Cease Striving**

Lord Jesus,

Our culture stresses endless activity. Help me to grasp the knowledge that a time of rest is not only a command, but also a gift from You. Today, allow me to understand it is all right for me to cease from continual activity in my life.

In Your name, I pray. Amen

My personality developed as a type "A." I set goals in my life. My to-do lists hang from the fridge. I specify, in my head, a date for when I want some chore, goal, or activity completed, and then I press on to complete it.

Because of this tendency, my life swirls in endless motion. The whirlwind of self-proclaimed demands leave me exhausted and irritable. Unfortunately, Sunday often becomes the day my volcano of tired grouchiness erupts. Why Sunday? After a long workweek, on Friday I cram in a romantic dinner date with my husband; Saturday, of course, is a chore day: housecleaning, grocery shopping, laundry, and assorted errands. Then Sunday morning arrives. We attend early service so my hubby can make it home to watch the early football game, NASCAR race, or golf. Since we are home for the day, it seems like a great time to clean the closet, write those belated thank you notes, bathe the dogs, or finish my Bible study. (Now, I realize this is self-imposed busyness. But I *need* to use those "free hours", don't I?) By Sunday evening, I am totally exhausted and dread the Monday morning alarm clock. So, I grumble about the busyness of my life, all that I still need to accomplish, and what wasn't done on the nagging "to-do" list. The next morning I crawl out of bed and put on my invisible "superwoman badge" to begin the wretched workweek all over again.

God never intended for life to be one long marathon of activities, whether secular or Christian. Because the malady of overwork and physical tiredness weakens our faith, we need to learn how to nurture and strengthen our faith by giving ourselves permission to cease striving all of the time. As we learn how to wait, our faith will flourish.

Can you relate? Briefly, describe a week in your life.

_____

_____

Mark below which creature best describes your life.
- ☐ Slug—do nothing
- ☐ Bear—hibernate for long periods
- ☐ Cat—work, but take catnaps
- ☐ Bee—work, rest, work
- ☐ Hummingbird—never stops

My life resembles a hummingbird—I never seem to stop. However, recently I heard the Lord whisper in my heart, "Cease striving." I knew the phrase was from Scripture, but I couldn't locate it. I searched and searched. Finally, I discovered the phrase in the New American Standard Bible. It is from Psalm 46:10.
Read Psalm 46:10 in your Bible and write it below.

_____

_____

Many of the versions read, "Be still". Actually, that is the one I am most familiar with; however, I believe the Lord wanted me to put "cease striving" into practice. How would you define the difference between the two phrases?

_____

Faith Fiction
God desires us to work tirelessly in kingdom work.

To me it seems "cease striving" implies to stop pushing and straining toward a goal. "Be still," says, "wait patiently." The Lord wants me to "cease striving". When I get on a roll in my walk of faith, I become a "career Christian". Everything I do seems to be a frantic effort to please God. Performance of my faith overrides my relationship with Christ. No wonder I heard, "Cease striving."

Our relationship with Jesus should always take precedence over our faith-based activities. Nonetheless, we can become confused as we read various passages on how we should act as Christians. View some passages that have the potential to provoke us to strive in our faith.

Read the following verses from James and note what they emphatically state.

James 2:18 _____

James 2:20 _____

James 2:26 _____

"Faith without deeds is dead." "Show me your faith without deeds, and I will show you my faith by what I do." These passages do indeed tell us to do good deeds so others will see and recognize God in us. The problem arises between working for our faith or our faith working for the benefit of others. The answer is to seek God's wisdom and direction as we walk in faith. Usually, this means waiting patiently for God to direct, rather than rushing ahead of Him with our agendas. Have you ever said yes to a task before seeking the Lord's direction? If yes, describe the physical, emotional, and spiritual toil that resulted.

Author David Roper describes our spiritual burnout as, "We try to be all things to all people all the time. We string ourselves out, expending all our time and energy, adding our will to God's, trying to do extremely well what he never intended for us to do at all!"[3]

Read the following verses from Psalms in your Bible and then fill in the missing words. _____*for the LORD; be strong and take heart and* _____*for the LORD.* Psalm 27:14

_____ *for the LORD and keep his way. He will exalt you to inherit the land; when the wicked are cut off, you will see it."* Psalm 37:34a

I _____ *for the LORD, my soul* _____ *, and in his word I put my hope."* Psalm 130:5

Waiting on the Lord seems like a waste of time in our culture of hurry, hurry, hurry. In Hebrew, *wait* (qāwāh) is a verb defined "as to wait, to look for, to hope for. The word is used to signify depending on and ordering activities around a future event."[4] Learning to cease striving equates to learning to wait on God's purpose and timing. Author Andrew Murray writes,

> Rest, then, and wait. Seek not only the help or the gift, but seek *Him*. Give God glory by resting in Him, trusting Him, and waiting for Him . . . It lets God *be God* . . .Whether it is in the designated periods of waiting or the continuous habit of the soul, rest in the Lord, be still before Him, and wait patiently. You will inherit the land—and all else that God has planned for you. [5]

In what areas of your life do you find it hard to "cease striving" and just wait?

_____

Describe how you could begin to wait on the Lord.

_____

Read Isaiah 40:31.

As we close today, take a moment to apply Isaiah 40:31. Ponder and then note how this verse could affect your faith on a daily basis if you began to cease striving and to wait on the Lord.

_____

Reread Isaiah 40:31. Then below, apply the various phrases to specific areas of your day-to-day life. Write down what you are expecting and hoping for today. Also, jot down what makes you weary and tired.

But those who wait for the Lord [who expect, look for, and hope in Him] shall change and renew their strength and power; they shall lift their wings and mount up [close to God] as eagles [mount up to the sun]; they shall run and not be weary, they shall walk and not faint or become tired.

Isaiah 40:31, AMP

I am waiting for the Lord [expect, look for, and hope in Him].

- Expecting and hoping for _____

- Weary and tired _____

My strength and power will renew and change.

- Expecting and hoping for _____

- Weary and tired _____

Faith Fun
Cease striving. Tear up your to-do list for today and wait for God to direct your activities.

I shall not be weary, faint, or tired.

- Expecting and hoping for _____

- Weary and tired _____

I shall mount up with wings of eagles.

- Expecting and hoping for _____

- Weary and tired _____

Finally, wait on the Lord. Meditate on Isaiah 40:31 and Psalm 46:10. Seek God's direction.

Father God,

In Jesus' name, Amen

Faith Finale!
Cease striving and know that I am God;
I will be exalted among the nations, I will be exalted in the earth.
Psalm 46:10, NASB

Day 4 – **Wilted Faith**

Lord God,

I don't understand why sometimes after my greatest moment of faith, my faith falters. It wilts like a flower in the desert. Teach me how to recognize this cycle and help me to learn to rest after my faith exceeds my emotional and physical resources.

In Jesus' name, Amen

My favorite moments occur when I am experiencing a closeness with God—a spiritual high. As author and speaker Beth Moore declares, "There ain't no high like the Most High!" My spirit cries out a hearty, "Amen!"

However, on the other side, my darkest days of depression follow after experiencing a feeling of closeness with the Lord. After a church retreat, a conference, or even a moving time of prayer, I am charged with happiness and enthusiasm. Then divine delight diminishes and dissipates. It's as if someone poked a pin in my helium balloon. My highest highs sink to the lowest lows. Fortunately, or perhaps unfortunately, many people experience these spiritual spirals. Mother Teresa, Oswald Chambers, and Charles Spurgeon, all mighty warriors for God's kingdom, experienced the melancholy meltdown. It comforts me to know that even the best get depressed.

Can you relate? If yes, can you describe a time you tumbled from a spiritual mountaintop to a valley of melancholy?

_____

Thankfully, God knew we would need encouragement. So often, we feel all alone, but in today's lesson, we stand side-by-side with others who have wilted faith.

Read 1 Kings 18:20-39. Then place a T for True or F for False by the following statements.

_____ Elijah came with many other prophets.

_____ Elijah challenged prophets of Baal to a spiritual dual.

_____ Elijah ordered buckets of water to be poured on the sacrifice to the Lord God.

_____ Elijah prayed.

_____ Fire came down and consumed both sacrifices.

_____ The people fell prostrate and cried "The LORD—he is God!"

Well, that would call for a faith-filled, spiritual high! Elijah displayed his faith. He acted on his faith. And God showed up on the mountaintop in response to Elijah's prayer. However, just like me, Elijah contracted a bad case of doubt and despair after this monumental demonstration of the power of the Lord God. Let's read the follow-up.

Read 1 King 19:1-9. What did Queen Jezebel threaten? (verses 1, 2)

_____

What emotion did Elijah feel? (verse 3)

_____

What did Elijah do in response to his fear? (verse 3)

_____

What did Elijah pray? (verse 4)

_____

What did the angel provide twice for Elijah?

_____

Elijah feared and ran for his life. This took place after his "spiritual experience" on Mount Horeb. He prayed, "I have had enough, LORD. Take my life" (verse 4). Elijah was definitely dealing with a severe case of depression. An angel appeared and presented him with a cake of bread and a jar of water—not just once, but

Faith Fiction
A great faith experience always increases your faith.

twice. This implies Elijah was in dire need of sleep and nourishment. Author David Roper writes, "Being spiritual doesn't mean expending effort in contemplation and prayer; it may mean eating supper and hitting the sack . . . . No lecture, no rebuke, no chiding—only a gentle touch from one of the Lord's tender angels, awakening Elijah to find food and drink." [6]

Do you remember our Lord Jesus sleeping on the boat? Let's examine what had taken place prior to His nap.

Read Matthew 8:14-18. Then number the events in numerical order by their occurrence.

_____ Many who were demon-possessed were brought to Him.
_____ Jesus saw the crowd around Him.
_____ He healed Peter's mother-in-law.
_____ He drove out the spirits with a word.
_____ He gave orders to cross to the other side of the lake.
_____ He healed all the sick.

Jesus had an eventful afternoon. No wonder He was tired. He healed all the sick and drove out many spirits. It makes me smile when I read, "When Jesus saw the crowds around him, he gave orders to cross to the other side of the lake" (verse 15). Enough is enough, even for Jesus. Jesus understands that our faith wilts when we are worn out.

Read Mark 6:30-31. Briefly describe the apostles' activities and the surrounding circumstances.

_____

_____

What did Jesus say to them?

_____

Jesus said, "Come with me by yourselves to a quiet place and get some rest." He recognized the need of His disciples to rest because He knew how draining serving people could be. Now, let's go back to Elijah. Elijah was fed, watered, and rested. However, his depressed faith lingered.

Read 1 Kings 19:8-18. Jot down the question the Lord asked Elijah. (verse 9)

_____

How did Elijah answer the Lord God?

_____

Describe how you perceive his state of mind and faith. (verse 10)

_____

What did the Lord command? (verse 11)

_____

Describe what Elijah experienced. (verses 11-13)

_____

Paraphrase what Elijah experienced, his response, and the Lord's question in verse 13.

_____

_____

In my opinion, Elijah was physically refreshed, but was still spiritually wilted. The Lord God commanded him to go stand on the mountain in the presence of the Lord. (Another mountaintop experience for Elijah?) God was not in the wind or the earthquake, but in the gentle whisper. Elijah, probably resentfully, pulled his cloak over his face, went, and stood in the mouth of the cave. Again, the Lord God asked, "What are you doing here, Elijah?" (verse 13). Again, Elijah responded with his bitter faithless diatribe.

Read 1 Kings 18:15-21. How did God encourage Elijah in his faith?

_____

The Lord sent Elijah back the way he came. He needed to face his fears in reverse. God encouraged Elijah with the announcement of others who were faithful to the one true God. In addition, God provided an intern prophet, Elisha, for the discouraged Elijah.

I relate to Elijah. Often my faith shrinks after God does something spectacular in my life. I cannot explain why this happens. I just know it does. However, I rejoice in the fact that the Bible acknowledges this type of wilted faith. So, I know what I can do the next time it happens. I must take care of my physical needs—nourishment and rest. Then, I need to wait for the gentle whisper of encouragement from the God who understands my humanity because He experienced it too.

Although we may come down from a spiritual mountain top experience and plunge into a valley of human gloominess, Jesus presented us with a powerful promise of encouragement.

Read Matthew 11:28, 29 in the margin. In your own words, rewrite the words of encouragement that Christ gave to each of us.

_____

_____

Faith Finale!
Then, because so many people were coming and going that they did not even have a chance to eat, he said to them, "Come with me by yourselves to a quiet place and get some rest." Mark 6:31

Day 5 – Green Pastures

Lord Jesus,

I ask that You make me lie down in green pastures. Teach me exactly where the green pastures are in my life. Let me learn to relax and enjoy the lushness of Your blessings in my life.

In Your name, Amen

Come to me, all you who are weary and burdened, and I will give you rest. Take my yoke upon you and learn from me, for I am gentle and humble in heart, and you will find rest for your souls.
Matthew 11:28, 29

Faith Fact
Great acts of faith may cause exhaustion that can result in wilted faith.

Faith Fun
Pack a sack lunch with a few favorite foods: apple, cheese, and a peanut butter and jelly sandwich. Make a thermos of tea or other hot beverage. Place a blanket on the floor and enjoy the provision of God, rest in His love, and listen for a whisper.

The LORD is my shepherd, I shall not be in want. He makes me lie down in green pastures, he leads me beside quiet waters, he restores my soul.
Psalm 23:1-3a

121

"He makes me lie down in green pastures." This familiar verse resonates with feelings of peace and rest. I always visualize a meadow with a bubbling brook whispering to me—"No cares. No worries."

However, recently during a women's Bible study I attend, new images of this verse began to develop. We were studying Priscilla Shirer's, *He Speaks to Me.* One of the thought-provoking questions was, "What is your green pasture?"

As our group discussed the question, the following responses emerged:

"My children—I love being a mother," stated a mother who had lost a child to cancer.

"Bubble baths and reading for hours," replied a woman who serves in ministry.

"I like to crawl into bed at night—just resting and knowing the day is over," said a woman who teaches at a local high school.

These responses caused me to ponder "green pastures" for days. What classifies as green pastures? What are the attributes of things that are capable of restoring our souls? They certainly aren't always places of physical beauty and serenity. I believe green pastures vary with the individual, the season of life, and the quiet place God has chosen for us to enjoy life. If asked today, "What are your green pastures, Susanne?" I could say being a mother, bubble baths, great books, and crawling into bed anticipating a good night's sleep. I would add dining out with my husband, rocking my grandchildren, and taking an afternoon nap.

Green pastures are the times and places in life that restore and refresh our souls from the ordinary wear and tear of the daily grind. Jesus desires to lead us to places of quiet refreshment and away from the storms of life. However, we must look around our mundane lives to discover our local green pastures, and then scurry to the side of the Shepherd, so He can *make* us lie down in our green pastures.

Are you ready to unearth *your* green pastures? All right, my friend, let's follow the Shepherd and see where He leads us.

We will dissect Psalm 23:1-3. Read these verses from the *Amplified Bible.*

THE LORD is my Shepherd [to feed, guide, and shield me], I shall not lack. He makes me lie down in [fresh, tender] green pastures; He leads me beside the still and restful waters. He refreshes and restores my life (my self); He leads me in the paths of righteousness. Psalm 23:1-3, AMP

What does the phrase "The Lord is my shepherd" mean to you?

_____

The Hebrew word for *shepherd* is *râ `âh*. The definition includes the concepts meaning to tend, a companion, to make friendship with and to pastor.[7] My favorite part of this definition is the concept of friendship. The Lord is my friend. Read John 15:13-15. What did Jesus state about friendship with us?

_____

Read John 10:14, 27. What do these verses state about Jesus as our Friend?

_____

Read James 2:23. What did Abraham do to be qualified as a friend of God?

_____

How does Abraham believing God relate to our relationship with Jesus as our Shepherd?

_____

Let's take this to a personal level. Why do you believe Jesus is your Good Shepherd and that you shall not lack for anything in His care? Explain your answer.

_____

_____

Are you a friend of Jesus? How do you display this friendship to God? Mark an X on the line below that best describes your ability to hear the call of the Shepherd?

_____

I need hearing aids   I hear a faint echo of His call   I hear, but don't listen   I hear and obey

Faith Fiction
God restores my soul only by religious activities.

Faith Fact
Jesus restores our souls by giving us enjoyment in small pleasures.

123

Jesus stated we are His friends. He declared Himself the Good Shepherd to His sheep. We are the sheep. The key is to we recognize and listen to Jesus' voice as He calls us toward green pastures. His provision will supply all our needs and we shall not lack for care.

Reread Psalm 23:2. "He makes me lie down in green pastures, he leads me beside still waters."

I find it interesting that He *makes* me lie down. He desires for me to enjoy the green pastures He provides for me. Then He leads me beside still waters—those quiet places where my soul finds refreshment and my faith is replenished. Obviously, most of us do not have a green pasture nearby. So the metaphor "green pasture" will mean something different to us. So, let's determine what our own green pastures might be. List ten activities or resources that produce relaxation, enjoyment, and contentment in your life--in other words, a green pasture. Your list might include anything from a furry kitten, to a toasted marshmallow, to a strenuous workout. What are the green pastures in your life?

_____   _____

_____   _____

_____   _____

_____   _____

As I mentioned earlier, my family, a bubble bath, and sitting in the sun on my patio with a good book tops my list of favorites. Your list might include hiking, shopping, cooking, your husband, your friends, or a good night's sleep. Whatever brings you pleasure and relaxation can be classified as a green pasture. So, if our pastures are so easily accessible, why does the Shepherd have to *make* us enjoy them? On the list below, check the obstacles that keep you from resting in the lush place of simple pleasures.

_____ Busyness   _____ Guilt   _____ Doubt
_____ Striving   _____ Dissatisfaction   _____ Pride

_____ Bitterness	_____ Anger	_____ Rebellion
_____ Indecision	_____ Depression	_____ Fear of failure
_____ Lack of trust	_____ Future achievements	_____ Stress
_____ Anxiety	_____ Commitments	

Read the following verses and underline the phrase telling why we should enjoy life. *Trust in the LORD and do good; dwell in the land and enjoy safe pasture.* Psalm 37:3

Moreover, when God gives any man wealth and possessions, and enables him to enjoy them, to accept his lot and be happy in his work—this is a gift of God. Ecclesiastes 5:19

So I commend the enjoyment of life, because nothing is better for a man under the sun than to eat and drink and be glad. Then joy will accompany him in his work all the days of the life God has given him under the sun. Ecclesiastes 8:15

Command those who are rich in this present world not to be arrogant nor to put their hope in wealth, which is so uncertain, but to put their hope in God, who richly provides us with everything for our enjoyment. 1 Timothy 6:17

Why does knowing and accepting the enjoyment of life help to increase our faith in God? For myself, it's evidence of His sweet provision in life. It's like a hug from His holy arms and a kiss of kindness to replenish my soul after the harshness of life strips away my smile. I am grateful for a Shepherd who tends to me in green pastures and offers me gifts of enjoyment and contentment.

Will you join me in thanking our Good Shepherd for making us lie down in our green pastures?

Sweet Shepherd,

Faith Fun
If it's summer, go to the park and lay in the grass. Enjoy the sunshine, the earthy smell of grass, and the laughter of children. If it's winter, sit by a fireplace in your home or in a restaurant with a cup of hot chocolate. Enjoy the warmth of the fire, the milky chocolate, and the dancing flames of light. Allow your faith to rest in the pastures of your Shepherd.

In Jesus' name, Amen

Faith Finale!

Trust in the Lord and do good; dwell in the land and enjoy safe pasture. Psalm 37:3

Faith Seed Thoughts & Prayers – **Review Week 5**
Journal your thoughts about how this week's lessons applied to you personally.

1 Zodhiates, Spiros, Th.D. Exe.Ed.& Baker, Warren, *Hebrew-Greek Study Bible*, (Chattanooga, TN: AMG Publishers, 1996), p. 1555, #8697.

2 http://www.ama-assn.org/amednews/2007/08/20/hlsa0820.htm.

3 *Taken from Elijah: A man Like Us© 1997 by David Roper. Used by permison of Discovery House Publishers Box 3566, Grand Rapids, MI 49501. All rights reserved.*

4 Baker, Warren D.R.E. and Eugene Carpenter, Ph.D.; eds. *The Complete Word Study Dictionary: Old Testament*, AMG Publishers, Chattanooga, TN; 2003. p. 986. #6960.

5 Murray, Andrew. *Waiting on God*, (Bethany House: Minneapolis, MN), 2003, 57.

6 *Taken from Elijah: A man Like Us© 1997 by David Roper. Used by permison of Discovery House Publishers Box 3566, Grand Rapids, MI 49501. All rights reserved.*

7 Baker, Warren, D.R.E. "Hebrew and Chaldee Dictionary," *The Complete Word Study Old Testament*, (Chattanooga, TN: AMG Publishers, 1994), P. 109, #7465.

Week 6
Birds in My Mustard Tree

Day 1 – **Unseen Treasures of Faith**

Lord Jesus,

I have studied the various truths about faith. I ask today for you to reveal to me the unseen aspects of my faith. Grant me the knowledge, wisdom, and revelation to perceive the birds that rest in my mustard tree of faith.

In Your Name, I pray. Amen

Secrets. Riches. Mysteries. Treasures. These words bring spine-tingling excitement. Around the world, *Pirates of the Caribbean* became an unexpected blockbuster movie. The Indiana Jones DVD series still, after over twenty years, sells consistently as a top gift item. Adventure novels prevail in the bestselling book lists. The hope of finding treasure enthralls us.

In this final week of our study, we are going to discover the treasures of our faith—birds in our mustard trees. Birds that roost deep within our faith tree are visible sometimes, sometimes not. We will go on a treasure hunt to find the secrets God reveals to us who seek Him in faith.

Read Isaiah 45:3. Then answer the following questions.
What will we find?

Where is it hidden?

_____

What purpose does the treasure hold?

_____

And I will give you treasures hidden in the darkness—secret riches. I will do this so you may know that I am the Lord, the God of Israel, the one who calls you by name.
Isaiah 45:3 NLT

God promises to give treasures—secret riches. He does this so our faith will be built on the foundation that He is the Lord and that He calls us by name. But what are these secret riches? What treasure can we find hidden in the darkness? Let's find out!

Read Proverbs 2:1-6. Fill in the blanks of the missing words.
My son, if you accept my words and store up my commands within you, turning your ear to _____ and applying your heart to _____ and if you call out for _____ and cry aloud for _____, and if you look for it as for silver and search for it as for hidden treasure, then you will _____ the fear of the LORD and find the _____ of God. For the LORD gives _____, and from his mouth come _____and _____.

After reading Proverbs 2:1-6, list the hidden treasures.

_____

Do these secret riches surprise you? Why or why not?

_____

How can these intangible treasures be of value to you?

_____

_____

Let's grab some more understanding about the treasures of faith God provides. Read the following Proverbs and note what you learn

Proverbs 1:7 _____

Proverbs 8:11 _____

Proverbs 9:10 _____

Proverbs 16:16 _____

Proverbs 24:4 _____

As we dig into God's Word, we find that wisdom, knowledge, and understanding are held in high regard. Their worth exceeds any monetary treasure we may gain on earth. Let's peruse a few New Testament verses to gain a greater understanding of these riches.

Read the following verses and then indicate which words you find in each by using the following:

A—Knowledge   B—Wisdom   C—Understanding   D—Revelation

_____ Ephesians 1:7-9   _____ Colossians 1:9-15
_____ Ephesians 1:17   _____ Colossians 2:2-3
_____ Philippians 1:9-11   _____ James 1:5

Examine the words *knowledge, wisdom, understanding,* and *revelation*. After each definition, note how the term results from faith and how it contributes to the increase of faith. Give an example of knowledge, understanding, wisdom, and revelation in your life.

Knowledge: *gnosis,* Objectively spoken of what is known, the object of knowledge and generally knowledge of doctrine, science, and religious knowledge.[1]

Results from faith:

Contributes to greater faith:

Faith Fiction
The result of great faith is always tangible.

Understanding: *sunéseōs*, To comprehend, to reason out. Comprehension, perception, understanding. The word denotes the ability to understand concepts and see the relationships between them. [2]

Results from faith:

Contributes to greater faith:

Wisdom: *sophía*, Skill in the affairs of life, practical wisdom, wise management as shown in the form of the best plans and selecting the best means . . . In respect to divine things, wisdom, knowledge, insight, deep understanding and includes the idea of practical application.[3]

Results from faith:

Contributes to greater faith:

Revelation: *apokálupsis*, Reveal . . . Spoken of the removal of ignorance and darkness by the communication of light and knowledge, illumination . . . The spirit of revelation means a spirit which can fathom and unfold the deep things of God.[4]

Results from faith:

Contributes to greater faith:

For myself, I have experienced knowledge by studying the word of God. We read this truth in Week One of our study. "So then faith cometh by hearing, and hearing by the word of God (Romans 10:17 KJV)." As I study Scripture, God grants me more understanding of His concepts and commands. Then, as I pray for and receive wisdom, I understand how to apply the concepts and commands to my life. The more I seek after knowledge, understanding, and wisdom, the more likely the Lord is to grant me "the spirit of revelation, a spirit which can fathom and unfold the deep things of God." As this cyclical process occurs, my faith deepens and grows. Wisdom, knowledge, understanding, and revelation become the evidence of my faith in Christ—birds in my mustard tree.

Read the following verses from Psalm 119, and then match the verse number with the correct phrase.

Psalm 119:18   Teach me knowledge and good judgment.

Psalm 119:34   Your word, O Lord, is eternal.

Psalm 119:66   Open my eyes to see wonderful things in your law.

Psalm 119:73   Give me understanding of your law.

Psalm 119:89   Give me understanding to learn your commands.

Psalm 119:105   Your word is a lamp unto my feet.

Scattered throughout Psalm 119 are the benefits of studying, believing, and living the precepts of God's Word. For me, the primary fertilizer for the growth of my faith has been the Bible. It teaches, scolds, and encourages me to walk in faith. As we close today, let's look at two verses in combination. Read the verses below and use each of them as the foundation for our closing prayer as we ask to discover the unseen treasures of our faith: knowledge, understanding, wisdom, and revelation.

What does the Scripture say? "Abraham believed God, and it was credited to him as righteousness." Romans 4:3

For what does the Scripture say? Abraham believed in (trusted in) God, and it was credited to his account as righteousness (right living and right standing with God). Romans 4:3 AMP

Every Scripture is God-breathed (given by His inspiration) and profitable for instruction, for reproof and conviction of sin, for correction of error and discipline in obedience, [and] for training in righteousness (in holy living, in conformity to God's will in thought, purpose, and action), So that the man of God may be complete and proficient, well fitted and thoroughly equipped for every good work. 2 Timothy 3:16-17 AMP

Faith Fact
The birds in our mustard tree of faith are often unseen by the physical eye.

Faith Fun
In a dark room, read Psalm 119 by flashlight or candlelight. Consider how God's Word illuminates your life in the darkness. His Word is the light for your life.

Lord God,

In Jesus' Name, Amen

Faith Finale!
My purpose is that they may be encouraged in heart and united in love, so that they may have the full riches of complete understanding, in order that they may know the mystery of God, namely, Christ, in whom are hidden all the treasures of wisdom and knowledge.
Colossians 2:2-3

Day 2 – **Extraordinary in the Ordinary**

Father God,

When I picture myself as faithful, I imagine myself doing great acts of faith. My deeds will be renown—"Isn't she faithful!" However, Father, teach me that faithfulness to You is found in the ordinary things of life. Help me to be faithful in the small tasks. Give me the wisdom to recognize the birds in my mustard tree are often small accomplishments of faithfulness.

In Jesus' Name, Amen

Biographies of Christians inspire me. I'll never forget finishing *Abandoned to God*, the true-life story of Oswald Chambers. Tears rolled down my face as I closed the back cover. I looked at my husband and said, "I want to be like Oswald Chambers."

He nodded absently, then patted my hand and replied, "Honey, you'll get a book published one day."

No! I didn't want to just write a book. I longed to live a life of total commitment to the Lord Jesus Christ. I wanted to travel to distant countries and preach the Gospel. I desired to have the faith Oswald Chambers had in every part of his life committed to God.

I want to do something extraordinary for God. However, I live an ordinary life of faith. My life looks like most middle-aged women in America. No inspiring biography will be written about my great feats of faith. My picture will not be recognized by anyone in one hundred years. Moreover, I am quite certain that a museum will never be built in remembrance of my achievements for Christ. No, I live an ordinary life of faith—but I long for the extraordinary.

Describe your life of faith. List the ordinary and the extraordinary achievements of faith.

_____

_____

_____

If you could achieve an amazing accomplishment of faith, what would it be? How likely is it to happen?

_____

_____

I believe we all want bigger and better outward displays of our faith. However, God looks at faith differently than we do. He looks at the purity and intent of our hearts. Today, I want to review obscure women who made the extraordinary list by being named in the Bible for their deeds. I highly doubt they would have ever thought their names and deeds would go down in God's Word for all eternity.

Faith Fiction
Great faith is exhibited only in great deeds.

Read the following passages and match the person with the correct act of faith and goodness.

2 Kings 4:4-38—A Shunammite	Taught the gospel of Jesus
Luke 2:36-37—Anna	A believer in Rome
Acts 9:36-41—Dorcas	Prayed and fasted in the temple
Acts 16:14—Lydia	Worked hard for others
Acts 18:24-26—Priscilla	Hospitality to Elisha
Romans 16:1-2—Phebe	Invited Paul to stay in her home
Romans 16:6—Mary	A servant of the church
Romans 16:15—Julia	Sewed clothes for widows

I love it! God honored the ordinary faith of women who did what they could with an attitude of humbleness. If I *could* sew and make clothes for the poor, God would think it was a mighty act of faith. However, I do volunteer at my home church. Hospitality comes easily to me. Hey, maybe I do extraordinary acts of faith and do not realize it!

Think about the women listed above and give five things you accomplish that God might consider great acts of faith.

1.
2.
3.
4.
5.

Let's move on to another verse that describes men who were ordinary, but who acted out their faith.

Read Act 4:8-13. Then answer the following questions.

What attribute did the rulers and elders first see in Peter and John?

_____

What did they recognize about the background of Peter and John?

_____

What did they "take note" of about Peter and John?

_____

The elders and rulers of the people saw the courage of Peter and John and were amazed by it because they recognized the two men were ordinary and unschooled. My favorite part of this passage is the phrase, "they were astonished and took note that these men had been with Jesus."

Being with Jesus makes us extraordinary. The Holy Spirit resides in us and people take notice. Let's look at another example of what God can do through a person who allows God to act through him.

Read Acts 14:11-15.
What did the people of Lystra believe concerning Paul and Barnabus? (Verse 11-13)

_____

How did Paul and Barnabus respond? (Verses14-15)

_____

Read Acts 19:11. Who did what through whom?

_____

We read these verses and say, "But that was the apostle Paul!" However, he was an ordinary man through whom God chose to work miracles. The works He does through us might seem less spectacular, but they are still miracles. For example, a tightwad Scrooge becomes a generous benefactor to the poor and needy. The recovered drug addict helps others turn toward God with their addictions. The high-strung mother becomes more patient with her toddlers. These are miracles straight from the nail-scarred hand of God. When we witness these miraculous changes in others or ourselves, we should praise the Lord for His mighty power working in us.

Read John 15:4 in the margin. How do we produce spiritual fruit in our lives—especially faith?

Abide in Me, and I in you. As the branch cannot bear fruit of itself, unless it abides in the vine, so neither can you, unless you abide in Me.
John 15:4 NASB

_____

In your own words, describe what it means to "abide in Jesus."

_____

Read 2 Corinthians 9:8. Explain what this verse reveals to you about your life, faith, and deeds.

_____

_____

I like Oswald Chambers' take on the extraordinary versus the ordinary in our lives. He wrote, "Suddenly Jesus appears to us, the fires are kindled, we have wonderful visions, then we have to learn to keep the secret of the burning heart that will go through anything. It is the dull, bald, dreary, commonplace day, with commonplace duties and people, that kills the burning heart unless we have learned the secret of abiding in Jesus."[5]

As we end today's lesson, consider your life with mustard seed faith that produces great deeds in the ordinariness of each day. We do not know whom we influence by small acts of kindness and goodness. Ponder the following praise by Richard Foster concerning his mother.

> So much about my mother was uneventful and ordinary. There was no spectacular drama, no newspaper headline, no high adventure. She lived an ordinary life and died an ordinary death.
>
> But she did both well. She loved my father well and loved us kids well. She lived through the drab terrain of the ordinary with grace and gentleness . . . My mother understood the sanctity of the ordinary. [6]

Extraordinary! Will you ask Christ to reveal to you your acts of ordinary faith that are truly extraordinary?

Lord Jesus,

In your name, Amen

Faith Finale!
And God is able to make all grace abound to you, so that in all things at all times, having all that you need, you will abound in every good work. 2 Corinthians 9:8

Day 3 – Harvest Time

Lord God,

I dislike waiting for the results of my prayer. I admit impatience hinders my faith walk. Doubt creeps to the surface when I do not quickly see answers. Help me to trust your wisdom and timing as you answer my prayers. Infuse me with Your Spirit as I pray in faith.

In Jesus' Name, Amen

After thirty-three turbulent years, she received the answer to her prayer. The years of verbal abuse finally ended. The violent fits of rage dissolved into a mixture of sweet kindness and mature patience. She planted prayers for more than three decades, and then suddenly God's response came. Finally, my mother harvested God's reply—her husband, my father, blossomed into a godly man. He died three years later.

Faith Fact
God sees small acts of kindness, goodness, and mercy as great acts of faith.

Faith Fun
Unscramble the names of the ordinary women whose faith was found to be extraordinary.

Ryma

Lajiu

Crodsa

Lilacpris

Behpe

Dilyia

The transformation of my mean Marine dad came as a complete surprise to me. I had given up on any hope of change in him. I tolerated him because of my love for my stepmom. The avoidance of interaction ruled our relationship. All this changed the day my stepmother experienced a bird in her mustard tree of faith—my father accepted Jesus Christ as his Savior.

On a crisp October evening, my dad lay on the bed, watching a rerun of a Billy Graham crusade. At the end, he walked out of the bedroom and said, "Kay, I need to pray. Help me know Jesus." At seventy-nine years of age, my father became a child of God.

Why did so many hardship-filled years pass before my stepmom, Kay, saw the results of her faith? I don't know. However, I do know it gave me a new perspective on learning to wait for the harvest of my prayers.

Faith Fiction
If we have enough faith, God answers our prayers quickly.

Are there prayers you are waiting to be answered? If yes, has the delay affected your faith?

_____

_____

God's timing is hard to understand. Today, we are going to explore Scripture with the purpose of keeping our faith while we wait for the Lord.

Read 2 Peter 3:8. How does this verse describe time from the Lord's perspective?

_____

But do not forget this one thing, dear friends: With the Lord a day is like a thousand years, and a thousand years are like a day.
2 Peter 3:8

How could this verse affect our prayers and faith?

_____

Describe your feelings about your unanswered prayers.

_____

_____

Well, we are not alone with our unanswered prayers. Throughout history, people have been disgruntled with God over His seemingly delayed responses. Let's examine the prophet, Habakkuk, who struggled with these same issues. (His name is a tongue twister, isn't it?) In the back of the Old Testament, look for the book of Habakkuk tucked between Nahum and Zephaniah.

Read the following verses. Note who is speaking and then paraphrase what is being said.

Habakkuk 1:12-13

_____

_____

Habakkuk 2:1

_____

_____

Habakkuk 2:2-3

_____

_____

Did you discover that Habakkuk is wondering why God is silent when treacherous people swallow up those more righteous than themselves? After asking this question, he declares he will stand and wait to see what answer is given to his complaint. God does respond, but does not give a definitive answer. The Lord declares, "Though it linger, wait for it; it will certainly come and will not delay." Then the Lord God goes further. He instructs Habakkuk, and us, with the ultimate answer.

Read Habakkuk 2:5b and then fill in the blanks below.
_But the _____ will live by his _____._
Thankfully, Jesus realizes it is difficult for us to wait, in faith, for God to respond to our requests. Let's see what He has to say about delayed answers.

Then Jesus told his disciples a parable to show them that they should always pray and not give up.
Luke 18:1

Read Luke 18: 1-8

List various circumstances in which you wonder when you will harvest the answers to your prayers.

1. _____

2. _____

3. _____

4. _____

Place an A, B, C, or D to note your discouragement next to the circumstance above.

A. No discouragement   B. Tad Bit Discouraged
C. Impatience with the delay   D. Despair and anger in the long wait

Rewrite the question Jesus asked in Luke 18:8b.

_____

How would you personally respond to His question?

_____

I can almost hear the sadness in Jesus' voice as He asked, "However, when the Son of Man comes will he find faith on the earth?" For myself, I know I had given up hope for the salvation of my own father. I believed God had given up on my dad too.

Read 2 Peter 3:9. What could I have gleaned from this verse?

_____

Is there someone you are waiting to accept Jesus Christ as his or her personal Lord and Savior? How long have you waited? Do you still believe it is possible?

_____

_____

Our faith may wane as we wait for answers to our prayers, for someone to receive Jesus, or for justice in an iniquitous circumstance. Thankfully, the Lord God understands. He gave parables, and of course, Habakkuk, to help our faith wait until the harvest. Let's find out what happened with Habakkuk and his impatience.

God spoke to Habakkuk in 2:20. What did He state as a reassurance to Habakkuk?

_____

_____

Read Habakkuk 3:16-19. List Habakkuk's responses in the correct numerical order (1-6).

_____ Heart pounded   _____ Rejoiced
_____ Waited patiently   _____ Strengthened
_____ Lips quivered   _____ Joyful in God

We should embed this idea into our own hearts because we want the Lord Jesus to find us faithful. Place your name in the blanks below and then close with prayer and a response much like Habakkuk's.

The Sovereign Lord is _____'s strength;

he makes _____'s feet like the feet of a deer,
               Your name

he enables _____to go on the heights.
              Your name

Lord God,

The Sovereign Lord is my strength; he makes my feet like the feet of a deer, he enables me to go on the heights.
Habakkuk 3:19

Faith Fun
Begin to journal your prayers in a notebook. Record how and when God responds. You will be surprised at the results. Keep your journal as a history book of your faith and God's faithfulness.

Faith Finale!

If it seems slow, wait patiently, for it will surely take place. It will not be delayed . . . but the righteous will live by their faith. Habakkuk 2:3b-4b NLT

Day 4 – **Future Sprouts and Baby Birds**

Lord Jesus,

I want to be made in Your image. When others look at me, I long for them to see a glimpse of You. I ask that as my faith increases, my family, friends, and co-workers' faith will increase too. Lord, allow their faith to sprout and to produce a mustard tree of faith.

Amen

Faith Fiction
My faith only affects my relationship with God.

An elderly husband and wife are sitting across from each other in a restaurant. A perplexed look crosses the man's face. He looks over at his wife of fifty-two years and asks, "Now which one of us doesn't like broccoli?"

Often when we share our lives with another person, we begin to become like that person. I can chat with a girlfriend over a long lunch and before long, I am using the same catch phrases and similar mannerisms. I meet with one friend for breakfast and we order the same breakfast for both of us: scrambled eggs, extra crispy hash browns, and multigrain pancakes. With another friend, I share the same taste in clothing. We have several identical outfits—we try not to wear them to church on the same day. My husband and I have become so similar that, like the elderly man, I want to ask, "Which one of us doesn't like broccoli?"

Although we cannot give our faith to anyone else, we can influence others with our faith. My prayer for my husband, children, grandchildren, and friends is that my faith might somehow help their own faith to blossom. Today we are going to study a few Scriptures that will help us to be intentional in our faith, so others might be able to produce a bit more growth in their own mustard tree faith.

List ten people you would like to influence by your faith.

1.   6.
2.   7.
3.   8.
4   9.
5.   10.

Let's discover how we let our faith shine into the lives of these ten people we listed.

Read the following verses and then describe how we could apply our faith in a similar manner.

Deuteronomy 4:9 _____

Deuteronomy 5:29 _____

Deuteronomy 6:5-7 _____

With whom are we to share our faith?

_____

In today's society, how do we primarily hear the "voice of the Lord" and "all the words of the law?"

_____

Concerning growing our faith and influencing others' faith, I see a trend of what we must do. Several times, over the past six weeks we have studied the precepts that we should love and revere the Lord, remember the lessons we have learned, and obey the commands He has taught us. The verses we read in Deuteronomy tell us to heed these precepts then our children and others that we care about will be influenced. Let's see what other instructions we can find in Deuteronomy.

Read the following verses and then fill in the blanks with the correct words. Deuteronomy 30:19 -20.

Now _____ _____, so that you and your children may live and that you may _____ the Lord your God, listen to his voice, and hold fast to him. For the _____ is your _____. Deuteronomy 30:19,20

They are not just _____ _____ for you--they are _____ _____. Deuteronomy 32:46-47

How would you explain these verses to someone?

_____

Now let's study how some biblical heroes conversed about their faith. Read Joshua 24:15.

Read Joshua 24:15 and 1 Corinthians 11:1-2. Describe the statement about their faith. Then mark an X to note how you think others would know about your faith in Christ Jesus.

Joshua 24:15 _____

I Corinthians 11:1-2 _____

_____

Unaware   Know I attend church   Know I am a Christian   Admire my faith in Jesus   See me as an obnoxious Bible thumper

When I first became a Christian, I carried around a sign in high school that said, "VOTE for JESUS!" I lugged a mammoth black Bible and made sure to place it on the corner of my desk. In hindsight, I was an obnoxious believer. Today, I have toned it down. People know I am Christian, but hopefully, I encourage them to seek Jesus for themselves.

My strongest desire in life is for my husband, children, and grandchildren to have a strong foundation of faith. I want the roots of their faith to grow deep, so when the storms of life blow through, their own mustard tree will stand firm. Listed below are verses that should encourage us as we share our personal faith with our families and friends.

Read the following verses and then describe how women can help sprout faith in others.

Acts 16:1 _____

2 Timothy 1:5 _____

1 Peter 3:1 _____

Colossians 1:3-6 _____

1 Thessalonians 1: 6-7 _____

In these verses, women of faith have the power to influence others. Our faith makes a difference in our husbands, children, grandchildren, friends, and even people we have never met. Our mustard seed faith produces sprouts and baby birds of faith. This brings us to our final lesson in *Birds in Our Mustard Tree*. Tomorrow, we will finish with discovering what *birds of faith*, actually do roost in our mustard trees. So until then, close today with a prayer asking the Lord to guide us in our ability to influence others.

Lord Jesus,

Faith Fun
Look through old photographs of family and friends. Call and thank the people who have had a positive influence in your faith. Pray for those whom you would like to influence with your growing mustard tree faith.

Faith Finale!

Love the Lord your God with all your heart and with all your soul and with all your strength. These commandments that I give you today are to be upon your hearts. Impress them on your children. Talk about them when you sit at home and when you walk along the road, when you lie down and when you get up. Deuteronomy 6:5-7

Day 5 – **Home to Roost**

Lord Jesus,

Thank you for Your Word in my life. My faith has multiplied over the past six weeks by my study of Your precepts and commands. Help me to keep my faith planted in You. I thank you that my faith has indeed increased. Thank you that I am able to recognize my faith in You.

In Your Name, I pray. Amen

My pomegranate bush reminds me of a Christmas tree decorated by the hand of God. Its branches hang heavy with crimson bulbs of fruit. It sways in the wind and I catch a whiff of the overripe fruit. Various types of sparrows and robins sit on the branches like "twelve partridges in a pear tree." Then I hear the high-pitched music of finches and hummingbirds beyond the lush fruit and deep within the branches. The birds on the exterior dance; the hidden birds continue to sing along in a bird chorus.

My pomegranate bush resembles our mustard seed faith that has flourished into a mustard tree with birds singing from its branches. Our faith has grown and today we will examine what visible and invisible birds of faith have come to roost. Let's begin by reviewing the past six lessons of *Birds in My Mustard Tree*. Skim through the previous lessons and jot down how your faith has increased because of your study of God's Word in each lesson.

Lesson 1 Mustard Seed Faith:

Lesson 2 Scared of the Dark:

Lesson 3 Amazing Faith:

Lesson 4: Broken Wings, Shattered Branches:

Lesson 5: Resting the Shade:

Lesson 6: Birds in My Mustard Tree:

I wish I could hear what you have learned. I have learned many things. But, I would say my primary focus throughout these past weeks has been to grow my shaky faith, one step, one hurdle, one circumstance at a time. Review in a new light a verse we have already studied.

Read Hebrews 11:1. Rewrite it in your own words.

_____

_____

We have learned that faith is not something we can necessarily see, hear, feel, taste, or touch. It is stepping out of our comfort zones and trusting God— regardless of how we feel emotionally.

List areas in which you feel out of your faith comfort zone, but you are relying on God.

_____

_____

Horatio G. Spafford wrote the familiar hymn, "It Is Well with My Soul" in 1872 when his four daughters drowned soon after his own financial bankruptcy. He, somehow, held onto the fact that despite the outward circumstances, God was good. He wrote, "And Lord, haste the day when my faith shall be sight." He knew his faith was not in vain, and someday he would see the meaning and purpose of all the tragedy surrounding his life at that moment.

For myself I think my greatest hidden bird of faith is the knowledge that God is good—*all the time*. Oswald Chambers wrote, "Faith by its very nature must be tested and tried. And the real trial of faith is not that we find it difficult to trust God, but that God's character must be proven trustworthy in our own minds."[7]

Faith Fiction
The results of our faith are always tangible.

NOW FAITH is the assurance (the confirmation, the title deed) of the things [we] hope for, being the proof of things [we] do not see and the conviction of their reality [faith perceiving as real fact what is not revealed to the senses].
Hebrews 11:1 AMP

147

God *is* good, even though I mourn with a dear Christian friend who lost a young son to cancer two years ago. Yesterday, her eighteen-year-old son was mugged and murdered. She asks, "Why?" I have no answer other than, "I don't know, but I cling to the factual knowledge that God is good, regardless." His goodness is a bird in my mustard tree of faith. Life is incomprehensible. However, Jesus is good and that knowledge sings from the depths of my soul. This bird in my mustard tree is more precious than life itself to me.

List a few of your "hidden birds of faith."

_____

_____

Our faith will grow into a great, sturdy tree where trophies of our faith will roost. However, there will always be moments of uncertainty. I find comfort in the words written by David Jeremiah in *My Heart's Desire*.

> You may sometimes feel awkward and uncomfortable, and find yourself saying, "Is this really true? I don't *see* anything in it. I don't hear God's voice. I don't feel His presence. There are days like that for all of us. The pursuit of God has no shortcuts. You simply must keep walking, keep seeking, and keep yearning. Keep at it, and you won't be disappointed. [8]

Read the following verses. Write the verses in the spaces below and describe how they are unseen birds of faith for your spirit.

Proverbs 8:17

_____

_____

Jeremiah 29:12-13

_____

_____

Nevertheless, what about the things that are evidences of faith we can see right now? The thrill of finding lost car keys, reading the perfect Scripture, your father receiving Jesus as Savior, your husband finding a great job, and the list can go on and on. Review the birds of faith that have come home to roost during this six-week study.

List some seen birds of faith in your mustard tree.

_____

_____

For myself, I think back to when my two sons were little boys. I began to pray for their future wives. So, I began a "shopping list" of prayers for daughters-in-law. It consisted of the following: godly, kind, sense of humor, good cooks, and fun families. Those prayers have been answered completely. I consider my "daughter-in-*loves*" to be two of the most evident birds to result from my faith.

What would you list as seen evidences of your faith?

_____

_____

If we combined our lists, we would be amazed at the variety of "birds" we would see. In the days and years ahead, we will see many more birds come to roost in our mustard tree of faith. We may never achieve "stained glass saints" faith, but we will keep on growing the seeds of our faith. We will keep pressing on toward the goal—Christ Jesus Himself.

Read Philippians 3:12-14. Describe how the process of pressing on in our faith could relate to these verses.

Now, let's let make the promise to press on in our faith. Pray and fill in your name in the blanks in these Philippians verses below.

Not that _____ have already obtained all this, or have already been made perfect, but _____ press on to take hold of that for which Christ Jesus took hold of _____. Philippians 3:12

_____ press on toward the goal to win the prize for which God has called _____ heavenward in Christ Jesus. Philippians 3:14

149

Now read Hosea 6:3. What is God's response to our promise to keep pressing onward in trust and belief?

_____

God will come to us. He approaches us even now. It makes my heart sing as I consider what thrills wait before us on this path of faith. Abraham Herschel described it as,

> Faith is not the clinging to a shrine. But an endless pilgrimage of
> the heart, audacious longing, burning songs, daring thoughts,
> impulse overwhelming the heart, usurping toward these are all a
> drive to love the one who rings our heart like a bell. [9]

As we close our study, I pray that it has encouraged you to keep continuing on in your faith. It is an endless pilgrimage of the heart. I have been blessed to share this journey of faith with you. I close with this benediction from the faithful apostle Paul,

Dear brothers and sisters, we always thank God for you, as is right, for we are thankful that your faith is flourishing and you are all growing in love for each other. 2 Thessalonians 1:3 NLT

Faith Finale!

What shall we say the kingdom of God is like, or what parable shall we use to describe it? It is like a mustard seed, which is the smallest seed you plant in the ground. Yet when planted, it grows and becomes the largest of all garden plants, with such big branches that the birds of the air can perch in its shade. Mark 4:30-32

Faith Seed Thoughts & Prayers – **Review Week 6**
Journal your thoughts about how this week's lessons applied to you personally.

Faith Fun
Draw a picture of a big bushy mustard tree. (It doesn't have to be a work of art.) As apples hang, write the names of birds of faith that roost in the branches. Also, on each branch write an attribute of God's goodness and faithfulness that you have discovered in this study.

1 Zodhiates, Spiros, Th.D., *The Complete Word Study Dictionary: New Testament*, (Chattanooga, TN: AMG Publishers) 1992. #1108, p. 378.

2 Ibid. #4907 p. 1342.

3 Ibid. #4678. p. 1300.

4 Ibid. # 602, p. 225.

5 Taken from *My Utmost for His Highest* by Oswald Chambers, edited by James Reimann, © 1992 by Oswald Chambers Publication Assn., Ltd., and used by permission by Discovery House Publishers, Grand Rapids MI 49501. All rights reserved.

6 Foster, Richard J. *Prayer: Finding the Heart's True Home* (New York, NY: HarperCollins Publishers, 1992), p. 170.

7 Taken from *My Utmost for His Highest* by Oswald Chambers, edited by James Reimann, © 1992 by Oswald Chambers Publication Assn., Ltd., and used by permission by Discovery House Publishers, Grand Rapids MI 49501. All rights reserved.

8 Jeremiah, David. *My Heart's Desire*, (Nashville, TN: Integrity Publishers, 2002), p. 203.

9 Heschel, Abraham. *Man Is Not Alone: A Philosophy of Religion,* (New York, NY: Octagon Books, 1972,), 174.

Note to Leaders

Visit www.randallhouse.com and receive a free Leader's Guide for *Birds in My Mustard Tree*. Discover tools to aid you in leading your group through a six-week study exploring the meaning of faith along with ways to have a growing faith. In this online resource you will find practical insights for group discussion and suggested extras for each week.

To order additional copies of
Birds in My Mustard Tree
Call 1·800·877·7030 or
log onto *www.randallhouse.com.*

Call for quantity discounts.

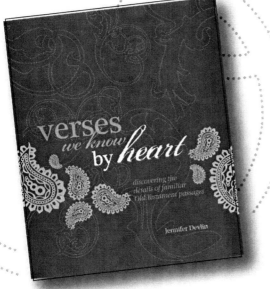

WALKING WITH MOSES
talking with God

$10.99

Group Discounts available!

10-ISBN: 0892656670

Moses was simply a man; a man of doubts, fears, faults, joys, triumphs, and defeats. His feet walked this earth more than 3400 years ago, yet the leadership lessons he learned along the way are just as relevant for each of us today. The example Moses set of hearing and faithfully answering the call of God is a lesson for all ages.

Walking With Moses—Talking With God is a small group study that will take students on a journey through the most significant events in the life of Moses as he finds himself leading the children of Israel. Situations lived by Moses will bring clarity to the path many others walk in following God; times of questioning, strange encounters, significant markers, and evidence of provision and protection. There are many lessons to be learned from the epic adventures in the life of Moses.

randall house

**To order call 1-800-877-7030
or visit www.randallhouse.com**

Printed in the United States
204933BV00003B/197-596/P

9 780892 656684